Praise for Stan Chambers

By TOM BROKAW

When I first arrived in Los Angeles in 1966, Stan
Chambers was already one of the star local reporters, and I
was immediately struck by his generous treatment us
newcomers. He'd help identify the newsmakers, he'd ask the
right questions, and he always left everyone feeling that they
were in the presence of a real gentleman.

Many years later, as I was nearing the end of my tenure
as anchor of *NBC Nightly News*, I was chosen to be the Grand
Marshall of the Rose Parade. And there to interview me, early
on that New Year's morning, was Stan Chambers—still
generous, warm, and always the gentleman. Moreover, he
looked like he'd put on maybe two years in the past thirty!
What do they have in the water at KTLA??

Stan, I am in awe of your career, and I am privileged to
have been your colleague.

All best, always,
Tom Brokaw

July 30, 2005

Dear Friends,

I am pleased to send my warmest wishes to all of you tonight as you honor Stan Chambers for his distinguished career spanning nearly sixty years in local television news.

Stan has contributed so much to Los Angeles over the course of his career. Actually, I'm surprise a national network didn't woo him away long ago. His dedication, integrity, and professionalism are legendary. Stan doesn't just report the news; he cares. And the Rose Parade just wouldn't be the same without him!

Congratulations, Stan, and I hope you all have a wonderful evening.

Sincerely,

Nancy Reagan

Society of Professional Journalists
A Tribute to Stan Chambers
Hilton Los Angeles/Universal City

KTLA's News At Ten:
Sixty Years With Stan Chambers

by Stan Chambers
with Lynn Price

Behler™
PUBLICATIONS
California
USA

Behler Publications
California

KTLA's News At Ten: Sixty Years With Stan Chambers
A Behler Publications Book

Copyright © 2008 by Stan Chambers
Cover design by Cathy Scott – www.mbcdesigns.com
Special thanks to Isabelle Chambers for her photographs

Library of Congress Cataloging-in-Publication Data

Chambers, Stan, 1922-
   KTLA's news at ten : sixty years with Stan Chambers / by Stan Chambers, with Lynn Price.
      p. cm.
   ISBN-13: 978-1-933016-50-4 (trade pbk.)
   ISBN-10: 1-933016-50-7 (trade pbk.)
   1. Chambers, Stan, 1922- 2. Television journalists--United States--Biography. 3. KTLA-TV (Television station : Los Angeles, Calif.) I. Price, Lynn, 1956- II. Title.
   PN4874.C424A3 2008
   070'.92--dc22

                              2007035382

FIRST PRINTING

Published by Behler Publications, LLC
Lake Forest, California
www.behlerpublications.com

Manufactured in the United States of America

Dedication

This book is dedicated to my great friend,
KTLA News anchorman Hal Fishman,
who died on August 7, 2007

Hal Fishman was a true television pioneer and the longest-running news anchorman in television history. Whenever Hal's dedicated audience wanted to get the full story of what was happening in their city, they tuned to KTLA to get his straightforward report.

Hal began his professional life as a political science professor at Cal State Los Angeles before joining KTLA in 1965. Even though he was no longer teaching, he believed in educating his viewers, and he often ad-libbed his reports to clarify a point or give background information.

Hal's strong sense of duty, high standards, dedication, and professionalism is a guiding light to those who follow. Having been his friend for many years, I feel the loss on a very personal level.

When I heard that *KTLA Prime News* was the most-watched show on the night we honored his passing, I swore I could hear Hal saying through a chuckle, "Stan, did you get a load of those high ratings?"

Hal, you were a major part of the exciting evolution of television news. Much of what I share in this book is your history as well. You were an icon, a great journalist, and a wonderful comrade.

I dedicate this book to you, my friend. Godspeed.

—Stan Chambers, 2007

Introduction
BY HAL FISHMAN

I've been anchoring the news in Los Angeles for thirty-five years. That must be some kind of record for longevity in a business known for its revolving-door policy on anchors and reporters. Nevertheless, when I started back in 1960, Stan Chambers had already been on television for thirteen years! He was there when it all began and is still there, reporting news in the morning and in the evening from all over Southern California. Viewers wonder if he ever rests.

The story of Stan Chambers is the story of television news. When Stan joined KTLA, Los Angeles was just beginning to emerge from its small-town mentality, and was viewed world-wide as some kind of lotus-land populated by retirees, citrus growers, and movie stars. Stan's career parallels Los Angeles becoming the megalopolis it is today. Stan was a television news reporter when the Big Red Cars traversed all of Southern California and trolleys ran along Hollywood Boulevard. And he was there as Los Angeles became the second most populous city in the country, capital of the Pacific Rim, and leader in aerospace and high-tech research and development.

Stan was also reporting to the people of Southern California during the tough times. Many readers will recall those powerful television images of the attempted rescue of little Kathy Fiscus. When you think about the Bel Air fire, the Baldwin Hills dam disaster, the Watts riots, the Sylmar earthquake, the airplane in the wires, the Laguna and Malibu fires, the Los Angeles riots, the Northridge quake, and a thousand other stories, you should know that only one reporter in the history of television covered them all, and his name is Stan Chambers.

Stan has also reported for us from Poland and Moscow. He covered the Pope's seventy-two hour visit to Los Angeles. He is known, recognized, and respected, not just locally, but all over the world.

This book is not merely a series of anecdotal presentations. It's essential and exciting reading for anyone who lives in Southern California and wants to gain a rare insight into their community and their own lives in relation to this vast multicultural society we call Los Angeles. It is also essential reading for anyone who watches television news anywhere in America. This book provides fascinating revelations about how news is gathered and presented to the public. After all, there is no more important source of information in our democratic society than television news, and the reader will find *News At Ten* a truly exciting book.

I can personally report to you that Stan Chambers is the same person off the air as you see on TV. His intelligence and boundless energy, his news judgment and professionalism, have helped make *KTLA Prime News* (formerly called *News At Ten*) the most successful prime time news program in the history of Los Angeles television. Most importantly, Stan is a true gentleman and deeply caring individual.

An inevitable result of being seen on TV every night is that so many people recognize you. And when you have worked as long and as closely with someone as I have with Stan Chambers, occasionally someone will greet me with "Hi, Stan."

Usually, I don't correct them—you see, I consider it a great compliment.

—Hal Fishman

FOREWORD

In January of 2007, KTLA started a full year of celebration in honor of its sixty years of television broadcasting. A live, three-hour KTLA telecast from the Roosevelt Hotel on Hollywood Boulevard kicked off a year-long party to recall those wonderful days when television was new.

This book is part of the celebration that offers a journey back in time to remember what a beacon of light KTLA has been for the past sixty years. We've come so far since those early days in 1947, when brand new television sets with their ten-inch screens broadcast live pictures from the outside world into living rooms all over Southern California.

Local television news is the people's news, the televised equivalent of the home-delivered newspaper, the day-to-day diary, the minutia of human activity that runs through our times. When you report the news in Los Angeles, you are broadcasting to the biggest hometown in the country with its nearly one hundred independent cities and communities.

We Angelenos have been through a lot together, from tragic riots to brush fires to earthquakes. And through it all, reporters and their camera crews record the stories in the field where the news is happening, and editors in the studios sweat against jaw-breaking deadlines of the evening newscast. Every night, through the choreographed chaos, we somehow overcome the stress, iron out the problems, and bring everything together for a near-flawless newscast.

Television reporters are an interesting breed. When something happens, we rush to the scene. With adrenaline pumping through our veins, we become the eyes and ears of a story, and I long ago lost count of how many times I've signed off on a report with the same words (and no small amount of pride): "Stan Chambers, Channel 5, News At Ten."

This is not a history, but rather a personal perspective drawn from my years of reporting. I have tried to recapture some of the past to show what it was like to be there at the beginning of television news, and how it evolved into what it is today.

Since I have been on the air for so many years, I often meet people who become misty-eyed when they talk about how they enjoy watching me on the news because I remind them of the days when their children were little and still at home. I often also meet those grown children, now with families of their own, who tell me I was one of the first people they ever saw on the TV screen when television was so new. I feel fortunate to be included in their television memories. Many were with me through good times, and quiet times, and times when things went wrong.

This business is about resiliency, a willingness to remain flexible and adaptable. I have been a local reporter at KTLA since just after it became the first commercial television station in the West in 1947. After sixty years, I like to think I learned a thing or two along the way.

-Stan Chambers

Acknowledgements

It has been a wonderful, rewarding, and nostalgic experience to revisit the past six decades of television broadcasting that have shaped our lives and times. There are many to whom I owe a debt of gratitude.

Our late KTLA News anchorman, Hal Fishman, was always an inspiration. He and I covered countless breaking news stories together, and I enjoyed spending time with him as we dusted off some of the lighter moments of our careers.

I want to thank my wife Gege, my eleven children, and their wonderful families for their unfailing support. I especially want to thank my son, Dave Chambers, and his beautiful and enthusiastic wife Deborah, for their creative collaboration and guidance. They helped bring the many treasured stories of my past back to life.

I am extremely grateful to Vinnie Malcolm, KTLA station manager, for his assistance, and to John Reardon, Tribune vice president, who has been a great inspiration and a wonderful friend these many years.

Many thanks go to my great friend and former news director, Jeff Wald, who was an ardent supporter throughout the writing of this book. I also offer special thanks to my new news director, Rich Goldner for helping me complete the later chapters. Jymm Adams, KTLA's creative services director, offered a lot of helpful advice as we neared completion. Tony Fote, news video editor, was tireless when it came to helping me find rich sources of news stories in the millions of video tapes that are in our electronic library. I would also like to say special thanks to news producer Gerry Ruben, assignment editor Vance Scott, and all my friends in the KTLA news department.

My publishers, Lynn and Fred Price, were magnificent through the long and demanding writing sessions. Lynn was a constant guide, who helped shape my memories into exciting stories.

Lastly, heartfelt thanks go to my grandson Jaime, who carries the Chambers tradition at KTLA into the future.

CHAPTER 1

The Thirties & Forties: Depression Days, Radio Days

I grew up in the mid-Wilshire section of Los Angeles. I attended St. Brendan's Grammar School during the 1930s and graduated from Loyola High School in 1941. I hardly remember my father, who died when I was four years old. My mother raised my brother Dave and me, working as an extra (and sometimes actress) in the motion picture industry. She would wake up early in the morning and dial the busy central casting phone number over and over, to see if they had any movie parts for her that day. During those difficult years, extras made three dollars a day. The Depression had a chokehold on the city, and twenty-five dollars a week was a good wage. You could buy a nice dinner for under two dollars, candy bars were three for a dime, coffee was five cents a cup, and malted milk and hamburgers cost about a quarter each.

We lived in a six story, middle-class apartment building on one of the streets that cross Wilshire Boulevard. The apartments were completely furnished, and they were painted and carpeted on a regular basis. The rent was about twenty-five dollars a month, which included linens and a weekly maid service. In a city that today is so dependent on cars, it's hard to imagine there were only a few back in those days. Most people took the streetcar or the bus, where tokens were three for a quarter.

At Mariposa and Wilshire, across from the Ambassador Hotel and its famous Coconut Grove, was the showroom for the sleek sport cars, the Auburn and the Cord. They were all the rage for those who could afford them. On the second floor, above the showroom, were the broadcast studios of the radio station KFAC.

This is where I made my radio debut. In 1937, my teacher at St. Brendan's, Mrs. Avis, produced a weekly children's program and used her students as the actors. About a dozen of us would go over to KFAC each week and perform in various children's dramas. It was exciting to be on the radio and hear our parents tell us how good we were. I vividly remember clipping the pages of my script onto pieces of cardboard just before airtime, carefully putting paper clips on all four edges of the script so that the paper wouldn't rattle during our live broadcasts. The fun part was playing many different characters during that semester.

I was entranced with all of the radio equipment, the studios, and the adults who had regular jobs there. I remember watching a sportscaster sitting in a small announcer's booth in the KFAC studio and broadcasting baseball games that were being played hundreds of miles away, with nothing but a Teletype machine. Someone at the park sent him a pitch-by-pitch account of the game on the Teletype, and it was the sportscaster's job to bring the game to life for the audience, using nothing more than tiny bits of paper and his imagination. The snap of the bat, the well-hit ball, and the sounds of the fans were all re-created in the studio.

Ronald Reagan was probably the most famous sportscaster to re-create the games. The future President was doing games in the Midwest about the same time that KFAC sportscaster was broadcasting the sounds of home runs in Los Angeles, and I kept thinking what a great job that would be. In fact, I used to re-create imaginary games alone in my bedroom. I cut out cardboard racing cars and pushed them around a racetrack on my carpet while announcing the races. If radio broadcasters could re-create sports events, I thought, so could I.

My radio was turned on every night, and I planned out my schoolwork carefully, so I could listen to the shows and do my homework during the commercials. *Jack Benny, Bing Crosby, Walter Winchell, Your Hit Parade, Amos and Andy,* and countless others were my constant companions.

By the time I got to Loyola High School, I had begun to enjoy public speaking. My first speech teacher, Father Doyle, was a rigid taskmaster. He insisted that we memorize everything and, most of all, pronounce every syllable of every word distinctly. I followed this with more speech classes when I went to Loyola University. I also wrote a column for the university but never considered journalism as a possible career.

The big change came when I joined the Navy's officer training program and was transferred to the University of Southern California for my senior year. We were encouraged to take a variety of electives to round out our regular courses, and I took advantage of the opportunity, appearing in a couple of college plays. Being on stage was a huge thrill for me, and I relished the challenges and pressures of performing. The smell of ropes and curtains, stored props, and mothballed costumes still trigger fond memories. The theater opened up so many other worlds.

This was my first experience with scripts, blocking scenes, and line memorization, and I loved the enthusiasm and rapport between cast members as we rehearsed in the weeks before opening night. This was a taste of make-believe that stayed with me during my Navy years.

I remember the June morning in 1944 when all of my newly-graduated classmates assembled at Union Station in downtown Los Angeles for a coast-to-coast train ride to Pre-Midshipmen School in Asbury Park, New Jersey. The newly constructed station was teeming with servicemen and families, everyone grabbing one last goodbye before we answered the roll call and boarded the reconfigured troop train for an uncomfortable five-day ride to Asbury Park. The military wasn't wasting any time — classes started the day after our arrival. We were going to be whipped into ensigns by the end of the year.

As we moved closer to graduation, a training officer just back from the South Pacific spoke to us about the big demand for fighter directors. The fighter director's job is to land on an island, carrying portable radio equipment, then find a high vantage point where he can see how the guns from Navy ships are doing against specific targets. Then he reports back to base, helping to direct the fire. Looking back, I still find it hard to believe that I volunteered to be trained for the position.

Upon graduation from my officer training, I received orders to report to Gulfport, Mississippi, for Aircraft Recognition School, the first step in my training. My days consisted of hours spent in front of a slide projector as various Japanese planes flashed on and off the screen, so I could learn to identify them. After several weeks, I became rather proficient.

In August of 1945, the country was startled to hear that a powerful new kind of bomb was dropped on Hiroshima, Japan. When the second bomb was dropped over Nagasaki, we knew the end of the war was at hand. I remember the boisterous and exuberant V-J Day demonstration down the streets of Gulfport. It had happened so fast, and I couldn't believe the war was really over.

My orders changed within a couple of weeks, and instead of Fighter Directors School in Hollywood, Florida, I was shipped to Newport, Rhode Island, to train the new crews being assigned to their ships. That lasted only a few months, and soon I received orders to go to the Naval Training Station in Bainbridge, Maryland, to prepare sailors for admission to the Naval Academy at Annapolis. I taught American History to the new students.

There were a couple dozen young ensigns on the faculty, and we all became friends. One of my good friends was the base supply officer, Ed Murtaugh, who played a mean game of baseball.. After one of our many after-hour games, we talked about our plans after we got out of the service. Ed's dad was a lawyer, and Ed hoped to follow in his footsteps at Harvard. Unlike Ed, my mind was far from being made up. I mentioned visiting a radio station in New Haven and how intrigued I was with the news operation.

Ed seemed to understand my interest. "I have a new unit that would be great for you, Stan. It's a wire recorder. You could practice your news broadcasting on it."

"A wire recorder? I know you can record on records, but I've never heard of a wire recorder."

"It's new," he said. "You talk into it, and it records your voice on a spool of thin wire. You can record over it as many times as you like. Come on over to my office later tonight and I'll show it to you."

Of course I took Ed up on his offer, and I was delighted. After that, I would bring a copy of the *Wall Street Journal* over to his office several nights a week and practice reading the news into his wire recorder.

Wire recorders didn't last long and were soon replaced by tape recorders, but that experience in Ed Murtaugh's supply office gave me a new sense of direction. However, before I started a broadcast career, I was going back to school.

The College Years

It was an exciting adventure to be in college in the late 1940s. Lives were starting all over again. I threw my discharge papers into a drawer and stuffed my uniform into my duffle bag forever. I was now a civilian, with a lot of hope for the future.

Just being on campus buoyed my spirits. And I wasn't the only one. There was a collective rush, a zeal that permeated the ivy-covered walls and rolling hills of colleges all over the country. The war was a thing of the past. All of the rigidity and restraint of the war years was broken. Dreams and opportunities could now become realities.

Getting a job wasn't even on my mind in those days. With the GI Bill, I just wanted to getting started being back in college. The new freedom of being on campus was thrilling after years of the military. I was no longer just a number and a member of a squad – I was finally my own master, judge, and trailblazer.

I was completely swept up in the creative atmosphere on the USC campus. I remember looking out of a fourth-story window of the Student Union building, watching the ebb and flow of the stream of students passing below, and feeling a surge of contentment, knowing I was a part of their parade. I belonged to the group. Each person down there had his own world to conquer and

I, somehow, shared vicariously in their adventure because it was my own as well.

I still hadn't made up my mind about my major, though I thought law school was my best bet. Under the GI Bill, I could sign up for almost anything, so why not law? I told everyone I was going to try it, and the encouragement I received helped me make up my wavering mind.

The Providence of Long Lines

Just like today, registration day was chaotic then. As I walked down busy University Avenue, past the cool shade of the Doheny Library, I saw a long line ahead of me at Bridge Hall. I stared at the massive single-file line pouring out of the front door, wrapped around the outside of the building. With a sinking feeling, I realized that was the line for the Law School. One of the promises I had made to myself after getting out of the Navy was that I'd never stand in another line. In the service it was always "hurry up and wait," and it always involved a line. The line for law school was too long, so I made a quick and illogical, decision; I didn't need law school.

And so, my law career was over before it even began.

I was thoughtful as I walked around the campus that day. The quiet, small campus I remembered from before the Navy had changed and grown considerably, and I knew I had to change with it.

My momentary setback was short-lived when I saw one of the old 1890s Victorian buildings on a side street. It bore a small, makeshift sign that said KUSC-FM. After my Navy experiences, the idea of majoring in radio broadcasting seemed interesting. So I met the professor in charge of the program, Dr. William Sener, and it seemed like this might be for me. Just to be safe, though, I decided to minor in radio broadcasting while working on a master's in history.

The radio classes were exciting. They were like workshops: we read scripts, broadcast over microphones, produced radio plays, and were immersed in all the basics of the profession. Best of all, since Los Angeles was the radio production center of the nation, USC could bring the professional radio world into the classroom. Our teachers were the same men and women who wrote, produced, acted in, and announced the programs we listened to nightly. Since television was practically unknown at that time, radio was still the major source of entertainment. Our instructors were celebrities with successful careers, and they were great role models. They helped many USC students bridge the gap from the college campus to the world of professional broadcasting.

My Future Takes Direction

Art Gilmore was one of the best announcers in the business. His voice was known to everyone. But despite his busy schedule, he found time to teach courses at USC, sharing his expertise and insights with us. He was the perfect blend of consummate teacher and industry professional.

I took his courses because they were fun, and I enjoyed learning from him. I never expected to get a job because of them. The turning point in my student career came when Art told me I had the ability to make it in radio. I was thrilled beyond my wildest dreams. Here was one of the best in the business telling me I had a chance.

That one conversation changed my entire outlook. I no longer concerned myself with getting a job to make a living but, instead, I knew I wanted to find a job that would make me happy. I decided to go for a broadcasting career.

I remember being in the KUSC broadcast studio one night, listening to the talk show *Tonight in Los Angeles*. They were discussing one of the local television channels, W6XYZ, and how it was going to expand its broadcasting schedule from two to six nights a week. I didn't even know there were stations on the air in 1946, but I thought this would be an excellent time for me to come up with some program ideas for television.

I called W6XYZ from a phone booth next to the old Capitol Records Building at Sunset and Vine, just across from the old NBC

Studios, and spoke to Gordon Wright, the program director. To my surprise, he showed some interest in my ideas. He was too busy to talk right then because it was T-Day, a big television promotion geared toward KTLA's expansion to twenty-eight hours of broadcasting each week, and asked me to call back later. I didn't realize it at the time, but this was only six weeks after KTLA had become a commercial station. The door was open slightly, and I made my first overture to television.

I met with Gordon Wright a few days later, and he suggested that we do one show and think about the possibility of more down the line. My plan was to do a broadcast version of *Campus Magazine*, which I helped publish at USC. The idea was to interview UCLA's star basketball player, Don Barksdale, who was featured in the sports section of the magazine, and also include some skits. We went over the magazine page by page until we had outlined the first broadcast of *Campus Magazine*.

About twenty USC students who worked at the radio station or the magazine got involved in the whirlwind of rehearsals and deadlines needed to produce the half-hour show. It aired on April 3, 1947, and when the show was over, there was no doubt in my mind that I wanted to get into television.

By late 1947, KTLA had increased its programming schedule to thirty-five hours a week, and more staff was being hired as a result. Gordon Wright remembered my USC magazine show and called to see if I wanted to take a full time job in television. I started working at KTLA on December 1, 1947.

The World in 1947

Los Angeles was a different city in 1947. You could buy a brand new Ford for $1,700. The home of your dreams was waiting for you, with no down payment, in the undeveloped San Fernando Valley, for $12,000, and the interest on your home loan would be four percent.

Thousands of GIs who passed through Los Angeles during the war liked what they saw and decided to move in. The big population boom was about to change southern California. We still had a light rail rapid transit system in those years, but few people were riding it. Freeways were mostly on the planning boards.

In 1947, we were still five years away from having jet airliners and ten years from color television. This was before videotape, calculators, and other miniaturization that has revolutionized our time. It was before the Beatles, Elvis Presley, and Michael Jackson, before the electronics industry and expensive gasoline. Computers were bulky adding machines, the Dodgers were in Brooklyn, and the Giants were in New York.

Developers were just starting to build homes in the suburbs, complete with new household conveniences like garbage disposals and air conditioning. Because Los Angeles was earthquake country, no high-rise buildings had been built here. It was before pacemakers and heart transplants. Passenger trains ran on time. Clark Gable was king, and people went to the movies twice a week.

Few newsreels and news programs appeared on television. One Los Angeles station ran an ad promising to show film of news events no more than forty-eight hours after they occurred. The ad further claimed to "scoop even first-run newsreels in movie houses."

This was before live television broadcasts could be transmitted from New York to Los Angeles. It was almost two years from the time KTLA first went on the air until all seven Los Angeles stations were broadcasting commercially. In those days, it wasn't unusual for most stations to be on only five days a week. Program logs showed notations like, "No Saturday programming on KNBH, no Thursday programs on KTTV, and no Tuesday broadcasting on KTSL."

This was the world of television that I entered. I took the job just for fun, thinking it would be an interesting interlude until I found a "real job."

CHAPTER 2

The Forties: I Become a News Announcer

I remember the first day I reported to work. I slowly opened the battered door of the old garage that had been converted into a television station. The cavernous building was one big open stage. Studio lights dangled from weather-beaten rafters, and heavy curtains hung from the tall ceiling to the bare wood floor below. The sets and props were stored around the stage area, and two big lumbering cameras were connected to the control room by large cables that snaked across the floor. Just inside the door, several rows of folding chairs were set up for audiences.

The place was informal, and I was surprised to see that anyone could just open the front door and walk in. It didn't take long for me to feel comfortable standing in the big open garage, and it quickly became my second home. I spent more time there than anywhere else.

I was originally hired to work for Gordon Wright in production, but there was so much that had to be done, it wasn't long before my production duties became just one task in a very long list.

I began my mornings with the routine sheets for the evening broadcast. These sheets listed all the films, slides, commercials, studios, performers, and everything else that anyone needed to know to put the evening telecasts on the air. It was always changing, so I spent a good part of the day checking details and rewriting the routine, which I would mimeograph and distribute to everyone.

Along with those duties, there were phone calls to answer, letters to open, visitors to talk to, props to order, errands to run, coffee breaks to take at Oblath's Restaurant next door, and the necessity of keeping my eyes on the changing test patterns each day. Part of my afternoon was spent helping the stage crew get the evening shows ready.

We typically had one major set to create each night, and it wasn't unusual for us to scatter bales of hay around the set and construct a corral fence sturdy enough for Cottonseed Clark and his Western songs, or to build a complete living room set for Lois Andrews' Hollywood Reports. Joan Barton required an entire nightclub for her show. Risers had to be brought in and assembled to create areas of the club at different levels. There were nightclub chairs, tables, and dinnerware. Carpets had to be laid, wall decorations put in place, and railings anchored firmly to the temporary steps. I was never good at assembling jigsaw puzzles, let alone these complicated sets, and I was grateful to be helping rather than being in charge. Famous last words, right? One day my new boss, Klaus Landsberg, raced onto the set and told Jerry Madden, the set boss, that his crew had to go with him to Pasadena immediately to solve some big problem at the Rose Parade.

"Stan, it looks like this is going to be up to you," Jerry said. "Can you handle it?"

I swallowed my fears. "Sure."

After Jerry left, I stood in the middle of the empty garage with the props all around me and a deadline looming. There was no plan or pattern. I had helped put the set together three times before and memory was my only guide.

Juggling the various wooden risers, I felt an urge to run away. I couldn't believe everyone had left and that I was completely alone. Those terrifying moments were what might be euphemistically be called a learning experience. I learned very quickly that remote broadcasts like the Rose Parade take precedent over studio shows. The next thing I learned was that no matter who you are, what you know, or how little experience you have, in this business you were expected to do everything, and you had better do it well.

Knowing this, I put all the building blocks together, only to find that I had several pieces left over. But the set did look a *little* like the nightclub, and somehow the show got on the air without criticism. I hoped no one would find out about the extra pieces.

Almost Derailed By Kissable Lips

A few weeks later, my first real chance at being a broadcast newsman was very nearly derailed before it could even get on the tracks. The villain was the old iconoscope camera that had evolved from the first television patent filed by the German inventor Paul Nipkow back in 1884, and it proved not to be my best ally.

The control room was busy that night; an interview program was on the air. The director spoke softly into a small microphone, giving the cameramen the cues to move their bulky cameras to their predetermined spots. There was a small cluster of engineers around a monitor that had a close up picture of my face on it. They were perplexed.

"Why do they look so funny?" one engineer asked.

"Strange," another added.

"Kissable," chuckled a third, as he twisted a few control room dials.

Klaus walked out of the control room and opened the door leading to the studio just wide enough to stick his head through. He looked closely at my face. "Looks okay in here," he mumbled.

He stood motionless for a while, then opened the door wide and walked onto the set. He studied my lips as I went through my interview with members of the Australian polo team. He then walked briskly back to the control room and, once again, carefully examined a TV receiver. "He looks fine on stage, but his lips look like Betty Boop's on the monitor."

"He does have deep indentations at the end of both sides of his mouth," someone else said, while peering into the monitor.

"These old cameras do strange things, but that is the first time I've ever seen that," said another.

"That's too bad," Klaus said, shaking his head. "He wants to be on the air, and these interviews would be good for him."

The engineer twisted a few more dials. "There must be some adjustment or something we could do to correct it."

"We'll have the new image orthicon cameras next month," Klaus said. "That could make a difference."

"Those lips are sure strange looking," another engineer joined in.

"I'll just have to keep him off the air until then," Klaus sighed. "His voice is too high, anyway, too young-sounding. That's the trouble with these young people just out of school. They need more experience."

The wonders of science saved my chance at a television career. Thankfully, the new image orthicon cameras were in use by the time I had a chance to do another interview show. They saved me from looking like the cartoon character with big beautiful lips.

But while science could fix my lips, nothing could save my high-pitched voice, and this remained a concern to Klaus. At one point, the order came down that I was not to be used as an announcer. It was all right for me to be seen on camera, but I couldn't be just a voice over the air. So, apart from the way I looked on camera and the way I sounded over a microphone, it was an impressive start.

Our only regular announcer, Keith Hetherington, knew I wanted to work in the announcer's booth, and he always tried to help me. Often, when a long movie was running and the sign-off time was after midnight, he would let me take his place so he could go home early. I did it from time to time, after long hours spent on the stage crew. Klaus never objected. Gradually, I worked my way back onto the announcing schedule.

Everybody Chips In

Everyone working at the station in those early days wore more than one hat. The end of the normal workday didn't mean everyone went home; it meant that everyone had to get ready for the broadcast. All the daytime executives took off their business jackets and, with their ties still on, started doing one of the stage crew jobs.

They could be seen pushing dollies, running the mike boom, moving lights, bringing in props, and helping set up the various scenes. I was always impressed with how they transformed from executives to crewmembers. Only their ties flagged them as being different.

As our staff expanded, the executives were replaced, and it wasn't long before we had crewmembers working the stage jobs and putting on shows. Since I wasn't an executive, I still worked with them part time. I enjoyed working on the crew, but I always worried about ending up there for good. To avoid this, I took a page from the executives' playbook and left my tie and suit coat on. My aim was to make this a constant reminder to those in charge that I wanted to be in front of the cameras—not behind them. My plan evidently worked because I was soon transferred to the film and slide department.

The new job blended nicely with my production and operations assignments on the daytime schedule, and gave me a chance to be on the air at night. As I pulled out all the slides for the evening broadcast and put them in order, I reflected that my clothing was more suitable in the film and slide room than on the stage.

The new job was brief. Commercials were becoming important to the station, and before long I was moved into the sales department.

From Soup and Voice-Overs to TV Dinners and News

When I started in 1947, newscasts were about fifteen minutes long. Videotape had yet to be invented, so no recording equipment was available. The studio cameras were the only ones we had. There were no news crews for local film coverage, no editors, no cameramen, no sound men or reporters.

KTLA's newscaster in those years was Gilbert Martyn, a respected broadcaster who had been with NBC Network News for many years. He was also the voice of the Paramount Newsreel. If you were a casting director, Gil's tall, dark, and dignified appearance would have made him your first choice for the role of television newscaster. His resonant voice and ad-libbing proficiency always made things flow smoothly when he was on camera. When commercials hit the air, Gil was receptive to chipping in where needed.

Since we were now a commercial station, we considered it a prestigious accomplishment to have a fully sponsored newscast. When the Rancho Soups commercial was being developed, it seemed logical that Gil Martyn should do it. News purists today would be shocked if the anchorman suddenly stopped reading the news, picked up a spoon, sipped some hot soup, did the commercial, and then went back to his news report. Hard as it is to imagine now, it made perfect sense to us in 1948. The soup tasting was a central part of the commercial every night.

Gil had the dramatic flair of a newsreel announcer. In those days, newsreels were still the main source of the visual news that people watched in their local movie theaters, and they were as important to us as the feature film.

The new television news program was a blend of pictures from newsreels and voices from radio. We scored music over various news stories just the way the newsreels did. A sound engineer had several acetate records with various recordings of mood music on his round tables, and he'd select the appropriate background music for the news stories of floods, wars, and light features seen on the broadcasts.

Our only source of news film was Hearst Metrotone News, and one of my jobs was to help unravel the film clips of stories. The optical sound strip on news film in those days was difficult to copy, and the sound quality was very poor. Every time a print was made, it lost quality. By the time it got to the West Coast, it was often difficult to understand what the person was saying. To fix the problem, we used the silent footage, and Gil narrated over it. In those days, newscasts weren't expected to give the station big ratings. We presented the news because it was our duty to our viewers and the Federal Communications Commission. The idea of building big audiences through delivering the news was a foreign concept back then.

The newsroom consisted of three desks, three news wire machines, two typewriters, and a few files. There was also a temperamental vintage printer that looked like a relic from a stockbroker's office. One of my jobs was to try to make it work.

KTLA programming always began with a test pattern and background music. To make the static test pattern more visual, KTLA presented a news summary that viewers could read while they waited for the television programming that night. Here is where the old stockbroker's printer did the trick. I would rip the latest United Press news summary off the clattering Teletype machine, walk over to the printer's old keyboard and type out the news.

The archaic typewriter printed on a narrow ribbon of paper that was rolled up like film. After rewinding it and placing it on two rollers, I gingerly placed the ribbon in front of a pre-focused camera, and the news of the day would be broadcast into hundreds of homes in Los Angeles. It was a makeshift, homemade procedure, but it worked well most of the time. Occasionally, it would get stuck and just stop on the screen. At other times the paper would break and the silent newscast would unceremoniously end. But for the most part, it was a great idea.

Face Time

When KTLA News expanded into a "Final Edition" broadcast each night at 11:00, I finally got my chance on the air. The broadcast was a close-up of a talking head. Since there were no teleprompters when I started, we tried to have as much eye contact with the viewer as possible. This was challenging because we had to look down at our scripts throughout the broadcast.

The day we got a Teleprompter, I decided to give it a try. The crew used a heavy stage weight to keep the three-foot-high wooden podium secure on the camera's base. A special typewriter with large letters was used to type the script on teletype paper about the size of a roll of paper towels. The finished script, fifty feet long, would be tightly wrapped around the wooden rollers at the bottom of the teleprompter unit. The top roller was placed just under the camera lens. The trick was to tape and place the top line of the paper as close to the camera lens as possible, so that it looked as if the broadcaster was looking right into the camera. When I went on the air, a member of the stage crew would stand next to the camera and carefully pull the rolled paper up as I read from my script. Since everything was done manually, I was always aware that the paper might jam, tear, or wrinkle at a bad angle for reading. There was also the chance that the operator would get lost and not be able to find the place in the script that I was trying to read. I was terrified, but after the first couple of times, I could see it helped create the "eye contact" that is so important in news broadcasting today.

Another early news show I was lucky enough to get on was *Eyewitness*. It followed Gil Martyn's news each night, and it usually featured live interviews with people involved in that day's news. The difficulty was in getting newsmakers to drive to the studio at night to be interviewed live. Most of them had never heard of the program, and a lot of them didn't want to talk about their involvement in the news. We would try to get policemen investigating crimes, firemen who had been involved in major fires, lawyers with exciting court cases, local politicians, city officials, and private citizens who happened to be eyewitnesses to events. Who could have known back then that one day we would have our own cameraman, sound man, and reporters shooting news film for our evening newscasts?

Times Change and So Does KTLA

By 1948, young GIs just home from the war and their brides began to save enough to buy new ten-inch television sets. People stopped going to the movies as frequently and instead ate TV dinners and made television an intimate part of their lives.

Programs were limited at first. There were old movies, many of them British because none of the major studios would release their feature films to television, except old Westerns, cartoons, and kinescopes from New York.

As new television stations came on the air, they developed their own local live programs. Program schedules expanded rapidly, and the hosts of these shows quickly developed into well-known television personalities. Since Hollywood had the performers and entertainers, it was easy for them to switch over from movies or radio. No one was paid much in those early days, and many people were able to take advantage of these television opportunities because they had other, better paying jobs to fall back on.

While the work was exciting, it was far from glamorous. Despite the tremendous heat on the sound stage, there was no air conditioning for the crew and the performers. The only air conditioning at the station was in the control room that housed all of the important electronic equipment. It was humbling to know that you could operate a station with overheated personnel, but not with overheated equipment.

There was only one bathroom at the station, and it took a couple of years before we had the luxury of both a men's and ladies' rest room. Equally lacking in square footage was our newsroom, which wasn't much bigger than a large closet, situated at the end of a long hall at the back of the old garage building.

City building and safety officials worried about how people could get out of there if there was a fire. They insisted on having another door installed that would allow for a quick escape to the street outside. The problem was that the room wasn't large enough, and a regular door would take up too much space. After a lot of head-scratching and negotiating with the city, we were permitted to install a horizontal, four-foot-wide, drawer-like escape hatch, which could be opened only in emergencies. While we never had to use the door, it was always interesting to show it to visitors touring the studio, and see their expressions of disbelief.

KTLA Becomes a Winner

KTLA began receiving awards and accolades for their shows and television personalities. Mike Stokey, the star of *Pantomime*

Quiz, received one of the first Emmys in 1949. Another person to receive an award that night was Klaus Landsberg, manager of KTLA. He was quite the Renaissance man of television, and is probably the person whose career captures, most accurately, the pioneering spirit of the early days of television.

Klause was a one-man show. Although his main focus was on electronic developments and television transmissions, he ran the programming side of things as well. Being completely independent, he learned everything about running and programming a station. But it didn't stop there. Klause showed an innate understanding of his audience as well, which was highlighted in 1949 when he dispatched a live television crew to the scene of a dramatic rescue attempt, something that had never been done before.

It happened less than a month after the station became commercial. There was a tremendous explosion in downtown Los Angeles: an electroplating company had blown up, leveling many buildings. Klause managed to get his large, bulky cameras out of the studio and onto a truck, so he could set up a signal from the explosion site. While the cameras showed the devastation, Dick Lane and Keith Hetherington interviewed the victims and rescue workers, and, for the first time ever, the station broadcast the news report live. Little did we realize that the face of TV news had just changed forever.

A hard-driving perfectionist, Klause had an enormous capacity for creative work. He demanded the best from his staff. From the time KTLA became commercial in 1947 to the fall of 1956 when he died of cancer at age forty, Klaus's imprint on television had become legendary.

He had a knack for knowing what people wanted to see. He called Los Angeles "the biggest hometown in the country," and he programmed the station to play to that audience. As the number of people that owned television sets grew, his KTLA became the television station of choice for the vast majority. We were on our way.

CHAPTER 3
The Weekend Time Stood Still

In April, 1949, I was the emcee of a B'nai Brith luncheon at the Biltmore Hotel in downtown Los Angeles. After lunch, I gave my speech, and I had just introduced the featured entertainer for the affair when the phone rang. I couldn't believe it! Right in the middle of his song, the telephone was ringing at the maître d's table.

The headwaiter saved the day by picking up the phone. He put the receiver down, looked around, and began walking toward the head table, which was on the other side of the huge Biltmore Bowl. As he came closer, all I could think was how embarrassing it would be for the unfortunate soul who had to get up and answer that phone.

I watched over my shoulder as he walked behind the other guests seated at the table. He stopped right behind me. "It's for you."

I felt everyone's eyes searing into my back as I followed him through the crowd. Thankfully the song ended, and the guests' applause allowed me minimal cover as I wove through the tables, a warm blush on my face.

It was my mother. My mother! I felt a surge of anger and embarrassment that she had chosen this, of all times, to call me. How could she do this to me?

I picked up the receiver with a curt "Hello."

"Have you heard about the little girl who fell in the well?" she asked in an anxious voice. "The station is sending a remote crew there to televise it. You're supposed to meet them out there."

I rushed back to the head table and explained to the chairman that I'd been called by the station to cover a news story in San Marino. She had heard about the little girl falling into the well and was gracious about my leaving. "How are you going to get out there?"

The question threw me. "I don't know. I'll have to make some phone calls. But I have to get there right away."

She turned to her husband. "Can you drive Stan to San Marino?"

In a matter of moments, we were on our way.

The Scene

I saw our two KTLA remote trucks in the middle of a vacant field as we drove around a corner to the rescue site. Getting out of the car, I walked over to a huge excavation site about thirty to forty feet wide and very deep. A man was huddled inside, cutting a hole in the side of a pipe that was protruding from the center. Small clumps of dirt and rock continuously fell on him. About a hundred feet beyond the site, our cameramen pulled cables while Bill Welsh, the reporter, got ready to go on the air.

"Just in time, Stan," Bill said. "We'll be going on in about ten minutes."

"What's the story?"

"A little girl fell into that abandoned well last night, and they've been trying to dig her out ever since."

"Is she alive?"

"Yes. Her mother could hear her crying in the well right after she fell in."

Klaus Landsberg stepped out of the truck with cameraman Jimmy Cassin, who was carrying earphones and a microphone. "You made good time, Stan," Klaus said, barely breaking his stride as he made sure everything was ready for the broadcast. "This might be a long one."

Bill walked me back to the excavation. "They started digging the hole last night. It got deeper and deeper, and the sides began to slide and dirt kept pouring down on the guys working at the bottom. There's no shoring or anything to protect the men down there." He pointed to the well casing in the center. "Little Kathy—she's not even four years old—is stuck somewhere inside of that mess."

A sick feeling gnawed in the pit of my stomach as Bill and I put on our headphones.

"We're all ready," Klaus said. He jumped into the truck and sat in front of the control panel's television monitors.

Bill and I put our heads inside the unit and watched the drama unfold on the television sets in front of us.

"They tried digging that big hole," Klaus said. "That didn't work, so they're trying to cut open a window in the side of the well pipe to see if they can spot her. I'll have these monitors in front of me to see what's going on and I'll tell you over the earphones so you can describe it."

Bill and I went on the air about the time that O.A. Kelley finished cutting into the well pipe with his blowtorch. He peered through the window into the dark well below.

He yelled to the workers on top, "I think I can see something that looks like a dress, but it's too far down there to be certain. That's about it. I can't see the little girl."

The sides of the huge crater kept slipping, and dirt was pouring down at a steady pace.

"Hey, will you guys stop moving around up there?" he shouted. "That loose dirt is going to bury me."

"Let's get out of there, Kelley," someone yelled, "I'm afraid the whole thing might collapse. Come on up."

Faced with the possibility of a major cave-in, the plan to reach Kathy through the side of the pipe had to be abandoned.

Although progress was slow, Bill and I had many things to talk about as we tag-teamed between talking to the rescue workers about new developments and announcing those plans during on-camera sessions. The story moved slowly but dramatically as everyone kept hope alive of rescuing Kathy Fiscus within a few hours. Bill and I tried to keep an optimistic tone in our reports. I remember repeating several times, "Kathy's mother heard her crying in the well right after she fell in. Her rescuers believe that she's unconscious and oblivious to what's going on."

Klaus's shots of firemen turning a crank on a small air pump were especially poignant, and captured everyone's desperation to save little Kathy. When it showed on the air, I remained silent, letting the picture speak for itself.

Although Bill and I didn't know it then, word that KTLA was telecasting the rescue effort swept through the city. Thousands turned their sets on and became involved in the drama unfolding before their eyes. Circus thin men and contortionists volunteered to be lowered into the hole upside down to try to get her out. The opening was only fourteen inches wide, but they believed they could go down the pipe, reach her, and pull her back up. Plumbers, sandhogs, specialty miners, and others with varying experience volunteered to go down into the hole to get her out.

News of the rescue attempt was also picked up by the wire services and transmitted to major cities all over the country. It became an international incident. Newspapers in Stockholm, London, and Australia held the presses for news of Kathy. Radio stations kept interrupting their broadcasts to bring listeners up to date. Switchboards at newspaper offices and radio stations all over the country were jammed with calls.

This was one of the first times a television station cut into a film it was broadcasting, cancelled it, and went to the scene of a breaking news story. The evolution of extended television news coverage happened overnight in that open field in San Marino.

The last plan involved bringing in a huge earth-drilling machine to dig a new hole. The corkscrew burrowed deep into the ground and pulled up layers of loose dirt before driving a huge steel casing into the earth.

I vividly recall standing in the dust and dirt, feeling the ground rumble, and listening to one of the engineers outlining the plan. "We're going to hammer that casing about a hundred feet into the ground to a point below where Kathy is trapped. We have to get out all of the dirt inside the casing, then go down to the bottom and cut a vertical tunnel across, shore it up with timbers, and try to dig across to the well pipe where we can get her."

It was a brave and dangerous plan. It also meant that it would be a long time before they could hope to reach Kathy.

I remember holding the microphone and speaking into the camera, saying that no one was supposed to remain beneath the surface for longer than twenty minutes. Digger Bill Yancy had been down in the hot, cramped casing for more than two hours.

Klaus Landsberg agreed to drop a microphone on a cable into the opening, so the volunteers on top could hear the men working below. It also gave our viewers a powerful narration of what was happening at every moment. I remember the sound of a pick cutting into rock, and the scraping of the bucket against the side of the casing as it made endless trips up and down. Bill Yancy's off-key singing kept everyone's spirits up while he tried to break through the layers of rock.

On through the night, the rescue workers spelled each other in the deep hole, fighting off fatigue, cold, falling dirt, mud, and rising water. Listeners and rescuers were able to hang on to every word via the microphone that KTLA dropped down to the bottom.

Throughout the long ordeal, the bucket continued to haul up more sloppy mud and water from the depths. There was little new to talk about, and Bill and I felt very much alone. Klaus was still talking to us over our earphones, but so little was happening that it was hard to imagine anyone could be watching.

Dawn found me sitting in a pick-up truck for warmth. A small opening at the top of the driver's window allowed the microphone cable to squeeze through. I kept on talking about what was happening and what we thought would be happening next. I remember looking at the mike resting on my lap and wondering if anyone could possibly be listening at this time of the morning.

As Sunday morning dawned, the mud had been scraped away and they were able to go deeper into the ground. As I would learn later, few people went anywhere that Sunday morning. When they did, the question was always, "Have they reached her yet?" Special prayers were offered for Kathy at church services. Many people slept on the floor in front of their television sets. As the morning hours passed, more and more people turned on their sets and remained in front of them for the rest of the day. Not surprisingly, the sandhogs, that small group of mud-splattered volunteers who worked one hundred feet under the ground, became famous.

By six o'clock Sunday evening, I found it much harder to get information. Nerves were frayed, officials were grim and testy. For the first time, the microphone in the casing was turned off, and that was our last official contact with the men working below. No reason was given, but I was afraid things had turned for the worse.

Kathy's parents were nearby during the entire ordeal, and we made no effort to invade their privacy during the long hours. They, too, watched in silence.

In a bitter twist of irony, Mr. Fiscus had just returned from testifying at hearings in Sacramento about legislation that would require the cementing and covering of all open wells. He was a water company official, the same one that had sunk this particular well over forty years ago.

Throughout the day, numerous conferences took place among the officials. Bill and I were no longer allowed to speak to the men who returned to the surface.

As darkness covered the scene, Dr. Robert McCullock, the family's physician, was strapped into a parachute harness. Grim-faced, he held the parachute lines tightly with both hands as he was lowered down to the crews working on the bottom. He was down there for only a few minutes before being slowly pulled back up to the surface.

Bill waved me over and handed me the microphone. I watched him walk away from the scene. Los Angeles County Sheriff Eugene Biscaluz, who was in charge of much of the operation, asked Bill if he would go to the Fiscus home and tell them that Kathy had been found dead.

Klaus moved a camera into position, telling me over my earphone that there was an important announcement next to the rescue site. A small crowd of somber rescue workers walked towards the camera. Another family physician, Dr. A. Hansen, stopped in front of the camera and spoke to the crowd. "Ladies and Gentlemen, Kathy is dead and has been dead for a long time. The family wishes to thank one and all for your heroic efforts to try to save their child . . ."

Tired, dirty, beaten men cried. Sandhogs with forty and fifty hours of constant work behind them wept openly. Rescuers stood silent, heads bowed, unwilling to accept the news. The crowd of thousands was stunned at the loss.

It was several hours before they brought up Kathy's body, but the broadcast was over. There was no reason to stay. The volunteers had tried to beat time and save a little girl, but failed.

Bill and I were on the air for twenty-seven and a half hours of continuous broadcasting. Viewers watched the entire drama unfold and suffered the poignant moment when they were told that Kathy was dead. The only solace was the fact that she had probably died shortly after falling into the well, and likely hadn't suffered long in her prison.

It was especially difficult for the men who had tried so hard to save her. They had given their all for a little girl they never knew but now would never forget.

CHAPTER 4
The Aftermath of Kathy Fiscus

In January of 1994, I opened a crumbling scrapbook on the top shelf of a dusty attic closet, filled with old letters, yellowed newspaper clippings, some telegrams, and pictures. Many had been pasted to the loose pages of the scrapbook my mother had put together after the telecast forty-five years ago. Carefully turning the pages, I was shocked by the vivid memories of that tragic weekend when an army of volunteers tried to rescue three-year-old Kathy Fiscus.

Historians in 1994 agree that the Kathy Fiscus telecast marked the beginning of the long form of television news coverage. It has long been recognized as the first important news event of the commercial television era.

Television in Los Angeles in the spring of 1949 was something you heard about at the office or saw in the window of an appliance store. Klaus Landsberg's decision to televise Kathy's rescue attempt brought the new medium of television to the general public of Southern California for the first time. It opened the window of the world to many viewers.

This old scrapbook has some of the letters I received after that marathon broadcast. They show the impact the telecast made on the viewers those many years ago.

Stewart Stern of Los Angeles wrote:
. . . We had been to a party. We sat on the floor in our tuxedos and watched you through the night and into the next night. Until that night, the television set was no more a threat to serenity than any other bit of furniture in the living room. Now you have utterly destroyed this

*safety forever . . . you and the epic which you have been
a part of this weekend have made us know what television is for. You have made many of us know that we
belong to the world. Through your own dignity and
your recognition of the dignity of others, you have given
us a flash of people at their best, as we remember them in
the battle, or as I've just seen them at Negev outposts in
Israel. Many of us had seen you with your polite faces
and amiable voices, but none of us had known you until
the voices lost their amiability and the polite faces were
beginning to sprout beards, along with our own. You
will never be forgotten by those of us who saw you there.*

I opened a folded newspaper clipping of Owen Callin's
column in the *Los Angeles Herald*. It said he was a captive of the
binding emotion holding him to the screen. He wrote:

*One of the greatest advancements in Los Angeles
television occurred over the weekend when the
possibility of covering major news events was
demonstrated with convincing thoroughness. We doubt
if there is a television set in the area which wasn't at
some time during Saturday and Sunday tuned to that
San Marino pasture where little Kathy Fiscus fell to her
death.*

I picked up another sheet of newspaper, yellowed with time. It
was an article by Bob Stock in the *Sherman Oaks Sun*.

*In this reporter's opinion, KTLA's coverage of this event
was one of the greatest reporting jobs in the history of
television . . . certainly the greatest in the Southern
California viewing area.*

There were several others on crumbling paper. *The Fontana
Herald and News* wrote:

*Television grew up in a hurry last week. The masterly
reporting of the tragedy of little Kathy Fiscus, who fell
to her death in an abandoned well, and the subsequent*

rescue, was so graphically detailed by KTLA, as to beggar description.

An editorial in another local paper summed up the human involvement that everyone felt.

We were all a part of the rescue attempt because we were there experiencing it as the drama unfolded on television. It is a curious, sad and magnificent world we live in. A little girl falls down a well in California and the news sweeps across oceans, waking untold millions to eager, anxious sympathy. Men work doggedly for 52 hours, baffled, almost exhausted and in increasing physical danger, to free her. There is no talk of work hours, rates of compensation, bargaining agencies, or safety conditions. They just dig on relentlessly while thousands of miles away offers of help pour in along with suggestions and prayers. Kathy's tiny wail has been heard around the world. It speaks for the small victims of war, of famine, of man's inhumanity to man, in Greece, in India, in Berlin and Shanghai, in Harlem and Cairo. And dull though men's imagination may be, San Marino shows us once more, they have in them the ability to respond magnificently.

Daily Variety, in a special editorial by Editor Arthur Unger, said:

The greatest job for the development, progress and advancement of television was done by the crew of KTLA, who for more than 24 hours televised the attempt to rescue alive Kathy Fiscus. Klaus Landsberg and his boys will never realize the important feat they accomplished for the advancement of television by the spot news reporting and visualization they did.

As I thumbed through letters, clippings and crumbling newspapers, I was touched by the praise and support. The public and the press unanimously commended the station for making television history. The emotional effect on the community was staggering. It seemed as if all of Los Angeles stopped to watch the drama unfold. A hard-boiled city poured out its tears and silent prayers as brave men worked in dark tunnels trying to rescue a little girl.

Not only was the telecast a major stepping stone in television history, but it dramatically altered my life. Even though I had been at KTLA for almost fourteen months and had been seen on many different programs, I was unknown to almost everyone outside the small band of loyal KTLA viewers. Dick Lane, Bill Welsh, Gil Martyn, and Dorothy Gardiner were the personalities everyone knew. I was just another face who appeared on the screen. You would see me from time to time on news and magazine programs, remote telecasts, cooking shows, community parades, commercials, and program previews. I was the original "utility infielder."

Fate Steps In

I resumed my regular television assignments after the Kathy Fiscus telecast. Over the next few weeks, I received a lot of mail and phone calls. One such call was from Marie McLoughlin, a friend of mine from USC, who was now married to her college sweetheart and living on a ranch in Ventura County.

She was sitting next to her mother watching the Kathy Fiscus telecast from San Marino when her mother remarked, "Marie, look at that nice fellow on television. He is so concerned and so emotionally involved with the rescue. He must be a wonderful person."

Since Marie and I were friends, she invited me over to her house for dinner to meet her husband, Bob Thomas, and her sister Beverly, a first-grade teacher at St. Paul's School in Westwood. Beverly had recently broken up with her boyfriend and was at the ranch to spend some with her family.

Beverly and I met the following week, and I can still vividly remember everything about her that day. She wore a blue knit dress and had the softest, most delightful voice I'd ever heard. I'm not sure what captivated me first, her quiet, regal demeanor, the beautiful glow emanating from her face, or her eyes that always seemed to smile.

It was one of those meetings that can't be described. Everything was perfect. Poets talk of love at first sight, but I never believed it was possible. How could two strangers know they were made for each other? But those poets were right—there was never a doubt in my mind. All I had to do was convince Beverly.

We hit it off from the very start, and went out every night after I finished working at the station. It wasn't too long before Beverly became acclimated to the strange hours a television announcer has to keep.

We decided just a few weeks after meeting that we should get married right away. We were married at Our Lady of The Lake Church in Lake Arrowhead on May 21, 1949. We were a couple in love, and stayed that way until she died on February 4, 1989.

Not only did the Kathy Fiscus telecast result in my meeting Beverly, but it also radically changed my professional life. The favorable reaction was so great that, for a short time, I was thrust into the strange phenomenon of being a celebrity television news reporter. It was a new category many others would soon join, and it was my good fortune and honor to be one of the first there. Prior to the telecast, television celebrities were mostly entertainers. All of a sudden, I was getting the kudos, although it was television that really made everything happen. I didn't really deserve it, but because I was there in the beginning, I became quite well known.

Although my fame was fleeting, as it usually is, I enjoyed the bright splashes it put on my life. I was emotionally uplifted by the new status and recognition. I felt that after being in the KTLA news department from the start, training and paying my dues, I was finally a full-fledged member of Klaus Landsberg's team.

But at what point does a television personality become a television newsman? My transformation from performer to reporter was gradual. There is no greater learning experience than doing something over and over again. The fact that I had been on the air a hundred times made it that much easier the next hundred times.

The real-life exposure to the traps and attractions of live television molded me into an experienced performer who was reasonably at home with a wide variety of challenges.

I never had to be an actor and assume someone else's character. The secret of being a good television reporter is to always be yourself, and I was able to do this every time I went on the air.

This isn't to say that the transition was smooth. I took many detours before I found my desired path, since there was really no such thing as a television news reporter in those days. There were news broadcasters and news announcers, sure, but reporters were yet to come. But news was where my heart was, and every time there was a slight turn toward that direction, I tried to take advantage of it.

KTLA was small enough to give me a chance and large enough to make room for me. I made good use of opportunities that came along, and I was always around and available whenever anybody needed something done.

That doesn't mean that everything went my way. It was a bumpy road over the years. I took plenty of blows while I battled my way back to my desired course. There were times when I didn't fit into a specific situation and wasn't surprised at being left out. But that didn't mean I wouldn't be used the next time.

There is a time for everything, and I guess my mother's phone call proved that. She called at the right time, and I answered. It changed my life forever.

CHAPTER 5

The Fifties: The City At Night, Family Life, & Frosty Frolics

One of the programs I really wanted to do was *City At Night*, another of Klaus Landsberg's revolutionary ideas. He took his television cameras out of the studio every night to interesting places around Los Angeles, such as the See's candy factory where they made their chocolate candy, or an automobile plant to watch new cars roll off the assembly line.

When *City At Night* started, Keith Hetherington and Dorothy Gardiner were given the assignment. I was disappointed because it looked like such a great opportunity. They turned out to be great hosts, and I was kept busy doing other assignments.

I remember one particular *City At Night* broadcast in March of 1950, when Beverly and I were expecting our first baby. We were watching *City At Night* that evening, counting contractions and expecting to leave at any moment. The program dealt with Fire Station 27 in Hollywood, one of the biggest and best in the city. It had all of the new fire equipment, and the show was going to give us an inside look at the latest in fire fighting hardware, as well as a chance to see how firemen spend their time at the station. The program had all of the elements of a good visual show. However, moments after the show went on the air, the fire alarm went off. The firemen jumped into their turn-out gear and raced through the station to their fire engines. Everything and everybody went pouring out of the station. Only one chief and Dorothy and Keith were left. Their visuals disappeared in front of them toward some unseen emergency, but they did a remarkably good job in the big empty fire station.

Like the disappearing firemen, Beverly and I never saw the end of the telecast, either. Stan Junior was born the next morning.

Some years later, Klaus decided to expand the broadcast and shoot *City At Night* from two different locations each evening. I was thrilled when I was assigned to work as a co-host on one of them, with Ken Graue. *City At Night* came on the air an hour after I finished broadcasting another program, so I always had plenty of time to drive to the remote location where my segment would televise.

One night I was scheduled to do a live broadcast from the San Gabriel Mission, the oldest church in Southern California. Time was going to be tight with this segment, since I was scheduled to open the show. I finished my earlier show and started the drive to the Mission Church in San Gabriel. Somehow, I missed my turn-off and kept on driving. I went on for about twenty minutes before I realized my mistake.

I wheeled around, raced back, found the street, and parked outside the Mission. When I went in, Father Michael Montoya, the pastor of the church, was on the air, taking viewers on a tour of the museum. He had started the broadcast without me, and most viewers never suspected a thing. As soon as I caught my breath and regained my composure, I joined him on the telecast.

City At Night had the special dimension of being live, and that meant that anything could happen. When things went wrong, there was no escape, and you had to work your way out of them. Cables got stuck around pillars, cameras had to be lifted and tilted to get through doorways, or they had to move quickly to reach the next shot that was needed. Some people being interviewed talked too long and had to be diplomatically cut off. Others answered questions with nothing but a yes or a no, leaving us with very short interviews we had to ad-lib our way through. Sometimes an assembly line shut down in the middle of a live shot and the moving, visual element of the program evaporated before our eyes. There were no excuses; someone had to keep on talking until what went wrong was fixed.

Family Life

What a sweeping change our lifestyle went through after that first year of our marriage. Beverly was the perfect mother: giving, kind, understanding, patient, knowledgeable, and loving. She made everything so easy for little Stan and me.

We moved to Santa Monica Canyon, then to a house on the beach, and finally lived the rest of our beach days at 56 Malibu Colony Drive—the perfect spot for our growing family. Malibu was considered far out in the country in those days, miles from everything. It was just a small beach community with only a hint of its famous past. There were still stories of the movie stars who had lived in the Colony before the war, though, and some were still there. But for us it was quiet, private, and utterly enjoyable.

Our daughter Beverly was born in September of 1951, our next son, David, in 1953, and then Nancy in 1955. We were a happy beach family and rarely left Malibu except for work, visits to our families, and trips to the Lying-In Hospital in Oxnard where our babies were born. The fifties was a simpler decade, more family-oriented, more traditional than those that followed.

Frosty Frolics

In the early morning hours, the old, cavernous, wooden Polar Palace ice rink was a quiet place. Patches of soft gray fog appeared to have been created by special effects technicians as it swirled around the frigid room. Its hazy pattern was ruffled only by the whirling motion of a solitary skater or the front door swinging open.

As the skaters straggled in to take their private lessons, the slashes of their skates and the sounds of their solitary voices echoed throughout the vast rink. And then the timbre of the pipe organ's music seemed to shake the high ceilings as skaters rumbled around the rink, caught in the spirit of the moment, rushing, dancing, and skating as if the party would never end. These were the stars who performed live every week in *Frosty Frolics*.

The ice show quickly became one of the most-watched television programs in Los Angeles during the early fifties. Most of the performers featured on the show were veterans of the popular traveling ice shows that crisscrossed the country. Shows like *Ice Follies* and *Ice Capades* were on the road most of the time. By appearing on *Frosty Frolics*, skaters could continue their careers and cut down on the traveling.

It was an ideal situation for everyone involved in the show, and every Wednesday was "opening night" on Channel 5. *Frosty Frolics* went on the air in June of 1951. It was the fourth-most-watched television show in Los Angeles by mid-August, and went on to be a permanent fixture on KTLA's entertainment schedule for over four years.

By mid-September, *Frosty Frolics* was offered for syndication on kinescope coast to coast on Paramount Transcription. On October 3, 1951, it went live over the ABC Network. This was at the very beginning of national television. The microwave transmission from Los Angeles to New York had just been completed, and *Frosty Frolics* was one of the first to be shown on the East Coast.

Despite its popular and artistic accomplishments, *Frosty Frolics'* coast-to-coast network days were numbered. The show's sponsor went bankrupt after only four network broadcasts. The kinescopes continued, but the live, splashy national network run ended unceremoniously when the vitamin sponsor bankrolling the airtime went under. Sponsor cancellations were a frequent fact of life in those early days, and although they happened often, they were never easy to accept.

Despite its network defeat, *Frosty Frolics* continued its popularity. It was a big success in Los Angeles. If a skater fell, he had no choice but to get up and continue his routine. If a set tipped over or a prop broke, there were no re-takes. Every skater knew to make the best out of any embarrassing situation. The uncertainty began to play a small part in the show, and skaters would sometimes include fake slips in their routines just to get an audience reaction.

During the morning hours on the day of the broadcast, each skater would rehearse their routine by staking out a section of the ice to practice the jumps, moves, and other special techniques they would be using in the program that night. Later in the day, an informal rehearsal would be held for timing and positioning. Then it would be off to wardrobe, makeup, and the show itself.

The audience watching at home was made to believe that *Frosty Frolics* took place at the Alpine Hotel, somewhere in the green forests of a beautiful mountain retreat. In reality, everything came from the prop department at Paramount Studios. Fake trees and real plants, tables, chairs, red carpeting for a walkway on the ice, cloth flats that were used to make the side of the hotel, and banisters for the dining area were all hauled over to the Polar Palace in the afternoon as the stage crew created their Alpine Hotel.

The flimsy cardboard "stone" walls were sprayed with a paint gun by an artistic genius, Sherman Laudermilk. He bent, twisted, and cut the cardboard, sprayed it with fast-drying paint, and created settings that you couldn't tell weren't the real thing. His crew was also responsible for building verandas, walks, gardens, and a small pine forest around an outdoor restaurant setting. The tables bordered the ice stage where the show came to life.

This was a complicated live stage production. The crew wore ice skates, and the props were brought in on sleds or pushed across the smooth ice surface by skating stagehands. Several members of the crew were hired for their professional hockey playing experience. Most, however, were novices who learned to skate in record time.

KTLA received countless calls from viewers who wanted to know the location of the Alpine Hotel so they could make dinner reservations or spend the weekend there. It made for interesting conversation when the switchboard operator explained that the Alpine Hotel wasn't real, and was broken down and returned to Paramount Studios each night, once the show was over.

Those in the audience at the Polar Palace sat on the wooden bleachers that were normally used during public skating sessions. Part of the excitement was being selected to sit at the dinner tables that ringed the ice. About two dozen lucky audience members were escorted across the slippery ice each night to the tables on the veranda.

The Clothes Make the Skater

If the skating was the bread of *Frosty Frolics*, the lavish costuming was the butter. Since KTLA was owned by Paramount Pictures, we had access to their vast prop and wardrobe department on the studio lot. These were the vital ingredients necessary to dazzle the crowd and make each show a success.

The costuming for *Frosty Frolics* started in an old warehouse where history was hung up to dry. Uniforms from the old soldiers' home were folded up over here, sheiks' flowing robes stashed over there. In the far corner was elegant attire from the court of Louis XIV.

The warehouse, heavy with the smell of mothballs and leather, was a cornucopia of vintage clothes that hung on bare racks three and four levels high. Paramount's wardrobe department was the legacy of the thousands of motion pictures filmed on the lot over the years. When a picture was completed, the costumes were stored in the warehouse for use in future films. This was a precious gold mine for the skaters of *Frosty Frolics*, and I remember walking down the narrow, cluttered aisles, listening to the skaters talk about how a certain costume would be just perfect for a particular routine. The variety was almost limitless, and the skaters took advantage of all they could to enhance their acts. It was heartening to see those forgotten, unused costumes pulled out of mothballs and given a brief new life on the ice.

Clothes Also Make the Host

I was the host and emcee on *Frosty Frolics*. The ice skates, gray Eisenhower-style jacket, and bright scarf were from the Paramount studio's wardrobe, but the suit pants were mine. I always put in my regular day in the sales department, and when things quieted down over there, I walked the two blocks to the Polar Palace to go over my lines for the evening's show.

The format called for me to introduce each number as if I was introducing them to the audience sitting at the tables on the ice at the Alpine Hotel. Klaus liked to keep everything fast and brief, so I kept my introductions just long enough for the stage crew to make the necessary set changes for the next number. Once they were ready, Klaus would give me the cue through the stage manager and I'd wrap up my ad-libbed introduction.

Since I was the only non-skater on the program, Klaus thought it would be funny for me to leave my garden set at the end of the broadcast and skate to the center of the ice as best I could. The plan was that I'd finish my closing announcement and then slip and fall down on the ice. That would be the cue for the full cast of skaters to come on camera and skate in a big, freewheeling circle around me. I would just sit there on the ice and wave while the skaters whirled to the music and the applause of the audience. It became a trademark of the show.

While it was an effective way to end the show, it had its occasional drawbacks. The first broadcast of *Frosty Frolics* that went coast-to-coast ended a couple of minutes early. Since network timing was precise, I had to sit in the middle of the ice in cold, wet slacks—that were getting wetter by the second—and wave to the national television audience while the skating cast made circle after circle after circle around me. Those few minutes felt like forever, especially after smiling and waving for a ridiculously long time. Live television certainly had its less pleasant moments.

As the show went on, we tried to make my end-of-the-show routines a little more unusual. One night I jumped off a Jeep, made a perfect landing, and then skated a few feet, to the applause of the crowd. I didn't fall until I stopped to take a bow. I tried turns, whirls, and different movements to show how my skating was improving, but, somehow, I still fell every night.

The landings got harder and wetter. This all had another undesirable side effect of putting holes in the knees of my suit pants. These were the same pants I'd wear on sales calls for the station later in the week, and each torn knee meant my already limited wardrobe was down one suit. Finally, I decided not wear my good pants on the show. Live and learn, right?

Looking back at all the shows Klaus developed, *Frosty Frolics* was one of the most entertaining and innovative. Few would have been so daring at that time to rent a rink, put together such a large cast, create new stories every week, and know the entire production would come together at airtime. Klaus had confidence in what he did, and he knew the show would come off. I feel fortunate to have been a part of that production.

CHAPTER 6

Return of the Marines, an Atomic Bomb and an Earthquake

Sitting high atop the hills overlooking the San Diego Harbor, gale-force winds whipped around my old Lincoln, shaking it throughout the night. I was half asleep in the front seat, and Beverly was asleep in the back, nestled under an overcoat. It was the summer of 1951, and this telecast was something KTLA had promised our viewers more than a year ago when we showed the Marines boarding ships bound for Korea. It had been a bitter war, far more brutal than we had expected. But now the war was winding down, and today our boys were coming home.

When Klaus caught wind of the ships returning to San Diego, he vowed to put up his own television microwave transmission link to cover the arrival. He held a series of long sessions with his chief engineers, Charles Theodore and John Silva, and they planned to set up several locations on mountain peaks where the signal could be relayed over shorter distances. As they got into the details of the effort, they discovered that a single relay station could do the trick from a windy peak on Point Loma.

Beverly and I had driven to Point Loma late that night to be with the crew when the preparations for the telecast started in the morning. Our mobile unit was stationed on the dock where the ships would tie up. The signal would be sent up to Point Loma via the link and then relayed back to our main transmitter on Mount Wilson for the broadcast.

San Diego is well over a hundred miles from Los Angeles, and it required precise, accurate engineering to transmit a signal over such a distance. Nothing like this had ever been done in

Southern California before. In 1951, it was a daring engineering feat to attempt something as complicated as this. So many things could go wrong, but Klaus felt we had to do this telecast.

Beverly and I drove down to the harbor a little after daybreak to get ready for the telecast. The bunting was up in red, white, and blue, and a huge WELCOME HOME banner waved in the breeze. The Navy band had arrived in buses, and instruments were being unloaded and tested. Hundreds of family members had gotten there early, and there was a feeling of jubilation as the crowd grew, waiting for the three ships coming home from Korea.

The Navy officials were very cooperative with our camera crews and offered to let us go aboard one of the ships before it entered the harbor. There was no way we could get a camera aboard, but Klaus took them up on their invitation anyway. He gave remote engineer John Polich a sound transmitter to haul out on a pilot boat and take aboard the troop ship. The heavy, bulky unit was the size of a large suitcase, but John tucked it under his arm and climbed the ladder to the deck of the ship, while hundreds of happy Marines cheered him on. KTLA talked to the combat veterans on the troop ship while cameras on the dock showed the faces of the waiting families.

It was an emotional telecast. Bands played soul-stirring marches as tears of joy filled the eyes of everyone on the dock. This broadcast was further proof of how well Klaus Landsberg understood the television audience. He let them share in the great emotional moments of the time. He involved them in the spectacle and let them experience the moment as it was happening.

Viewer feedback was so positive and enthusiastic that Klaus scheduled another, similar telecast a few months later. For that telecast, Dick Lane and I were surrounded by thousands of people as we stood under a hot November sun on a crowded Navy dock, scanning the horizon just beyond the breakwater. We wanted to be among the first to spot the cruisers, *Helena* and *Toledo*, when they came into view. The ships had left Long Beach the previous July and had been in action off Korea for many months. Now their long wartime tour was over and they were coming home for good.

KTLA went on the air at 11:30 that Wednesday morning, and it was a full three hours before the welcome home party was over and the telecast went off the air. There was little that Dick Lane and I needed to say over the air. The pictures told the story. The cameras panned the crowd and caught the suspense, the excitement, and the raw emotion. We provided just enough commentary to tie things together as we waited for the ships.

The cameras' long lenses showed the crew members standing at attention on the decks of the cruisers as they neared the dock. Many of the shots were too personal to comment on. They showed the pure embodiment of love, and that was enough. The young bride seeing her husband only a hundred yards away said so much more than anything I could have added. It was more important that the viewers reacted to what they saw, rather than listening to excessive description from us. Klaus believed the unfolding of great drama in which people were caught up in emotion was television at its best.

Bob Hull, television critic for the old *Los Angeles Mirror*, praised KTLA for its coverage of the arrival of the cruisers. He wrote, "The KTLA personnel handling the assignment are to be complimented. There were moments when Dick Lane and Stan Chambers on the microphones could have been maudlin in their commentary, but they were smart enough to let the viewers' own emotion react to what they saw, without giving any verbal prompting."

The extra efforts that went into those broadcasts helped build the KTLA reputation. When Klaus decided something was of vital importance and had to be televised, there was nothing that would stop him from getting it on the air. Programming would be thrown out, commercials cancelled, and the station would concentrate exclusively on televising the big story.

With the success of the microwave link set up for the San Diego broadcast, Klaus knew KTLA could duplicate it almost anywhere. He'd proven that long distances wouldn't interfere with the station's coverage, and the stage was set for other ambitious engineering efforts.

KTLA Scores With the Atomic Bomb

Those were great years of experimentation and innovation for KTLA, and 1951 was one of the best. KTLA continued to be different. Viewers had Channel 5 locked in on their television sets and were watching the station in great numbers. In January, KTLA programs took nine of the top fifteen spots on all the rating services. In March, seven of the top ten most-watched programs were on KTLA, and in August, all of the top eight shows were ours.

In 1951, a series of atomic bomb tests were scheduled to be done in the Nevada desert. These events were top secret, and there was little a television station could do to show them. But Klaus Landsberg decided he would try anyway. Experts predicted that the light from the test blast in the Nevada desert would be seen all over the West for several hundred miles, so Klaus decided to go live with a telecast in the early morning hours to capture it.

There was no way of getting close to the bomb test site since it was restricted. Gil Martyn was sent to Las Vegas for an audio report of what he saw. Dick Lane went to Mount Wilson with the only cameras for an early morning telecast of the detonation blast.

Dick Lane and Gil Martyn were on the air for about an hour talking about the bomb and what the viewers would see. They brought us right up to the countdown and the blast in the early morning hours in February 1951. When the bright light exploded in the dark eastern sky, it lasted for just an instant, but viewers knew they were the first to see a live atomic blast on television. A transcription of the coverage was donated to the Atomic Energy Commission.

When the rating surveys came out, they showed that over 30,000 viewers were up and watching that 5:00 a.m. broadcast. In 1951 that was a substantial audience. As usual, Klaus was right again.

In 1952, to satisfy the growing interest in the tests, the Atomic Energy Commission decided to permit live television coverage from the Nevada Proving Grounds. The project looked doomed right from the start. Network officials said they weren't going to cover the bomb test because it would be nearly impossible to get cameras to the site. Phone company officials had completed their surveys and determined it would cost more than $60,000 to set up a relay link to transmit live pictures more than 250 miles from the desert to Los Angeles. They also said they didn't have enough time to construct the microwave system before the scheduled blast.

Klaus Landsberg was astounded that the networks would pass up covering this historic event. He offered to take over the project and put up his own microwave network to assure the coverage would take place. He planned to place television-transmitting equipment on desolate mountain peaks between KTLA's transmitter on Mount Wilson and the test site at Camp Mercury in the Nevada desert. He had less than a month to do it.

The available equipment was large and bulky, and there was almost no way to get it to the mountaintops to set up the communications link. Klaus spent hours poring over maps, selecting peaks that might be used as transmission sites to relay the signal. He worked closely with his KTLA crew to gather everything he needed for the broadcast, and then flew to Las Vegas to check out possible sites firsthand. The survey showed that he had a good chance of pulling it off, with one exception: there was an unmarked, inaccessible mountain in the middle of the Nevada desert, a key relay site that was necessary to make his plan work. Unless he could get his bulky equipment to the top of it, he wouldn't meet the deadline or get the coverage. There seemed no way he could get his gear up to the 6,500-foot level on the uncharted mountain. His attempt to televise the test was getting a lot of publicity and everyone was rooting for him, but he had almost reached a dead end.

The only way to get the equipment to the top would be with a helicopter, but who at that time had helicopters that could carry that much weight and fly that high? Klaus's answer was the Marines at the El Toro base. He phoned the commanding officer, told him about the problem, and asked if they would be interested in tackling such an innovative operation. This was something the Marine copters had never tried before, but the Marine chain of command started working and the answer came back a resounding yes. Klause was jubilant. Now his television link had a good chance of being completed. He pulled out all the stops, put the station on the back burner, and took his crew to the Nevada desert.

Valley Wells, a small community near Mount X, became his operations base. All the gear necessary for the relay system was hauled up there from Los Angeles. The Marines flew up two big helicopters and planted them on the flat, dusty desert at Valley Wells. Klause was optimistic, although the job was another one of those television firsts that no one had ever attempted before. Once all of the gear was gathered at the base camp, Klause tackled the task of flying roughly 12,000 pounds of equipment to the mountain peak. In 1952, Marine helicopters had never flown higher than 5,000 feet. Now they had to carry all that weight to a 6,500-foot peak in an unpredictable desert atmosphere that often created tricky flying conditions.

All the fears were unfounded. The copters took off with their heavy loads, easily climbed beyond the 5,000-foot level, and successfully airlifted the sensitive gear to the mountain peak. This included the big, eight-foot transmitting dish that had to be tied on with ropes and carried outside the copter because there was no way to get it inside. On successive flights, all four KTLA crewmembers, with parachutes strapped on tight, were flown up and deposited next to their gear on the top of the wind-swept mountain.

Klause worked around the clock with his crew to get the system operating. Mount X was the critical point because it was set to link up with Mount San Antonio in Southern California, 140 miles away. He had another link at the 9,000-foot level of Mount Charleston, about forty miles from the blast site.

The crews were spread out at the different transmitting sites and knew they were stuck there until the telecast was over. The desert was windy and freezing cold at night, with gale-force winds, giving way to blistering temperatures during the day. Campsites were quickly set up on the mountains, and everyone worked to get their part of the link operational. The crews used familiar tricks like flashing lights on a regular basis to try to establish visual sightings between their transmitter sites on Mountain X, Stone Mountain, and Mount Charleston.

If this wasn't nerve-wracking enough, a sandstorm swept over the desert, threatening to do permanent damage to the relay equipment and put it out of commission. Mother Nature was threatening to disrupt the operation, but Klaus felt sure that he had the system established and that everything would work. He ordered the rest of the crew to leave Los Angeles and get ready for the A-bomb test.

Klaus kept the link operational by running it twenty-four hours a day until the blast test. There was always at least one engineer on duty and awake at each location, babysitting the equipment on the desolate mountain peaks. We had cameras stationed about ten miles away from ground zero. Those were prepared to capture the historic event as announcers Grant Holcomb and Fred Henry stood by for the broadcast on April 22, 1952. Even though Klause had set up the engineering side, the networks provided the pool program coverage televised to the nation. We were ready to go.

Cameraman Robin Clark had his Mount Charleston camera in position forty miles away, to give viewers an overview of the vast desert scene as the test preparations continued. His cameras would also show the mushroom cloud when the time came, and served as a back-up position in case anything went wrong with the relay.

That morning, reporters Holcomb and Henry were on the air from "News Nob," our desert perch from where we did our nationwide broadcasting. All eyes were on the sky looking for the Air Force bomber that would fly over the desert site and drop its load on the target.

Just before zero hour, a power failure occurred at "News Nob" and the cameras went dead. Klaus screamed at his crew, "What happened? Where's the picture? Somebody get out there and fix it!"

Several engineers rushed from the makeshift control center to the desert floor to look at equipment, cables, cameras—anything that could be fixed in the next ten seconds.

Robin, on the backup camera, watched the drop plane. Because of the power failure, he had no communication with anyone as he carefully tracked the target. At the precise time of the scheduled drop, he pulled back to a long shot and centered on the area where he thought the blast would be.

He couldn't know it at the time, but Robin wound up getting the only picture that reached the transmitting link. The tremendous blast exploded in the desert sky, right in the center of Robin's camera, forty miles away. Moments later, the power failure was corrected, the primary cameras came back on the line, and the coverage continued. Most people watching thought that Klause had cut to the long-shot camera to show how the atomic blast dwarfed everything around it.

Thirty years later, Robin is a successful motion-picture producer, and he told me that he still looks back with pride on that remarkable moment when he saved the telecast of the first atomic bomb blast in the Nevada desert.

(After the broadcast ended, our job still wasn't over. All the camera and relay equipment needed to be taken off the mountains. One of the big Marine helicopters had trouble landing on a mountain peak. It bounced off one of the large boulders and fell on its side. Thankfully, no one was hurt by the spinning blades, but all of the gear the copter had hauled up for us had to be hand-carried down the mountain by the KTLA engineers.)

The telecast was historic in every respect. Once again, KTLA was showered with accolades, awards, commendations, and nationwide industry respect. The AEC had another test the following week, and KTLA was granted permission to televise it from Mount Charleston where Robin and his camera were stationed. This was an all-KTLA telecast. Gil Martyn and I were the reporters for the broadcast, and it was a thrilling experience to be part of such a momentous television event.

Klause, ever the showman, always believed in taking advantage of situations. Since the relay link from Las Vegas to Los Angeles was still in place, I flew back again the following weekend with the KTLA crews to do a live broadcast of the annual El Dorado Parade from downtown Las Vegas. After all, why not do another live special from out of state and show that KTLA was there?

The Tehachapi Earthquake

My family's beachfront home in Malibu was built on short stilts. When Santa Ana winds blew out of the canyons behind us, the raging force rattled windows, overturned patio furniture, and battered the house with such fury we could almost feel it shake. But that wind was nothing compared to the battering our house took from an earthquake the morning of July 15, 1952. The crescendo of creaking and rumbling jarred us awake, and each shudder of the house seemed like it could be the final one that would tear it apart.

As Beverly and I made our way to the children's rooms, the force of the earthquake sent us sprawling in opposite directions. This was the first major quake I had felt since the Long Beach earthquake on March 10, 1933, that had measured 6.3 on the Richter scale, causing widespread damage to Southern California and killing many. I would learn later that this quake measured 7.8. I feared the worst.

Amazingly, our home wasn't damaged, but I knew it was going to be a memorable day for me. Thankfully, metropolitan Los Angeles suffered surprisingly little damage, and we all hoped other cities would be as fortunate. It took a little time, but word began to reach our newsroom that there had been fatalities and considerable damage to the little mountain town of Tehachapi, not far from Bakersfield. As more information filtered in, we learned that Bakersfield itself had also suffered major damage.

KTLA quickly geared up for coverage of the disaster. A map check of Tehachapi showed that it would be almost impossible to televise out of there. We had never tried to get a television signal from anywhere in that area, but we were buoyed by the success of the atom bomb coverage less than three months before, and were determined to try to get cameras there.

Gil Martyn and I were sent with the crew to downtown Tehachapi to try to bring our viewers live coverage. It was a difficult job, due to the fact that the town was more than one hundred and fifty miles away and surrounded by mountains. Everything hinged on the telephone company's permanent installations and their ability to provide us with a link to Los Angeles. As usual, Klaus was the first to act, contacting the phone company to request a loop. It was brilliant planning on his part because, for the first time, there was competition from other stations. Executives had begun to realize the importance of live coverage after watching the atom-blast telecast, and a number of stations were starting to cover the news like KTLA did.

While our units drove to Tehachapi, all the stations tried to secure phone lines from the earthquake zone. Phone company officials decided they could set up only one television transmitting line to Los Angeles. Naturally, all of the stations wanted it, even though KTLA had been first to ask. Klaus broke the impasse by offering to share the link. Each station would get its share of time on the broadcast link from the earthquake site, but they couldn't go on the air until after KTLA. Channel 5 had equipment there early, and when the phone company opened up the line, we were again the first to report from the scene of a major news story.

The old 1910 buildings made from un-reinforced concrete sustained most of the damage, and several people were killed from falling brick and rubble that crushed their apartments and stores. Our reports in Tehachapi detailed the earthquake after it had already happened, and all we could do was broadcast the damage and clean-up efforts. Or so we thought. I was on the air reporting when I felt a rumble under my feet. The large aftershock wrenched me immediately from my comfortable spot as an objective reporter to the new role of a terrorized participant. I had trouble keeping my balance, but I knew I had to keep on talking and describing how the tremor felt. I still have no idea what I said, but to say I was relieved when the shaking stopped would be a serious understatement.

Cots and blankets were set up under the trees in a nearby park, and we spent that night under the stars. A religious group from Chatsworth arrived with clothing, food, and beds for everyone. I remember lying on a cot that night, looking up at the sky and thinking about how much I loved being a television news reporter and being in the center of things when they happened. It was a great privilege to be a source of information that helped people cope in troubled times. We could stop the rumors, dispel the fears, give the viewers the facts, and keep them up to date on the changing news of the moment.

Additionally, the Tehachapi quake telecast was very important because it reminded everyone that Southern California is earthquake country. Despite knowing how vulnerable we were, and that we could be hit again at any time, I slept well that night under the stars.

Times Are Changing

Even though KTLA beat out the competition at every turn, it only stood to reason that things couldn't stay that way forever. The networks had begun to make inroads to KTLA's near monopoly on the Los Angeles market, and Klaus knew that the 1952 Presidential election returns would have to be shared. Since the election returns were scheduled to be covered live on television, coast-to-coast, for the first time, the viewing audience was expected to be quite large.

Klaus knew he couldn't beat the competition at its own game, so he looked at the strengths and weaknesses of the other stations, and thought about what he could do to prevent losing his audience. The coverage on the networks would go on for hours, and the sheer size of it would capture the biggest share of the audience. Since there was no way his news staff could compete with the live election returns broadcast from all over the country, he decided to counter-program election night with a vengeance, with Ina Ray Hutton and her all-woman orchestra. Ina's show was KTLA's highest-rated show on Tuesday nights, and Klaus expanded the *Ina Ray Hutton Show* to two full hours that night, calling it *Election Jamboree*. It was a brilliant idea because Ina Ray was a successful performer, and her band was an entertaining contrast to all the male bands of the era. She received a great deal of attention whenever she played because it was unusual to see women playing saxophones, trombones, and clarinets, so she had a big following. Since there was a rule at the station that men didn't appear on her regular show, *Election Jamboree* would mark the first time that men would be allowed on the stage with Ina Ray.

Klaus stepped up the on-air promotion of KTLA's election night coverage by promising great entertainment, the excitement of an election party, and all the election returns. He had his news reporters—Gil Martyn, Jay Elliot, Tom Hatton, Ken Graue, and me—prepare for short cut-ins of the election returns throughout the night. It was a perfect match: we reporters gave election returns while Ina Ray Hutton provided music and entertainment.

The election turned out the way Klaus predicted. General Eisenhower jumped out to a big lead early on and remained there until the end. For all practical purposes, it was over early in the evening, but the other networks continued full coverage throughout the night to broadcast the governors' races in each state and local elections all over the country.

According to the ratings, *Election Jamboree* was a winner. KTLA received the largest viewing audience with their "Ike and Ina" combination and beat out all the other network and local stations. Once again, Klaus not only kept KTLA's head above water, but continued to create innovative methods to keep our audience interested.

CHAPTER 7

KTLA: First in the Air, First in the West

The aircraft carrier *Valley Forge* was anchored off the Santa Monica Pier on July 4th of 1953. The Navy and the city of Santa Monica had planned a big fireworks celebration, and thousands were expected to jam the park and the beachfront. It wasn't often that a carrier parked right off Santa Monica, and everyone involved wanted to make this event as memorable as possible.

When Klaus heard about the holiday plans, he decided to do a live show from aboard the carrier. The Navy brass liked his idea and gave KTLA the royal treatment. The broadcast would concentrate on the fireworks, but Klaus wanted to go a step further and show what life is like on a Navy carrier. To do this, the KTLA Telemobile, a self-contained, remote broadcasting unit that could be rolled on a moment's notice, had to be brought onboard the *Valley Forge*. Klaus's great idea very nearly became our undoing.

As the truck holding our camera equipment drove off the paved road and started across the beach to the tide line where a Navy-landing barge was waiting, it stalled and got stuck in the sand. The rear wheels spun, and it sunk in up to its hubcaps. Beachgoers got a good laugh watching the repeated attempts to get the television remote truck out of the sand.

The crew used boards, rocks, and even coils of cables to try to give the truck enough traction to dig out. Giving up, the four KTLA crewmembers got out and tried to push the truck free. The small crowd finally took pity and gave them a hand. Three or four people helped rock the truck forward as another half dozen took positions at the rear bumper and started to shove. Another dozen joined in, and finally they were able to push it across the soft sand. The crowd cheered while everyone pushed the truck to the surf line where the open ramp of the landing barge was waiting. The crew of the Navy barge slung a line around the truck and used a special rigging from a powered hoist to pull it the rest of the way. The can-do attitude of the KTLA crew, the beachgoers, and the Navy saved the day.

There were many invited guests on board the *Valley Forge* that night. Shore boats picked up the visitors from the pier and took them out to the decorated ship. Bill Welsh and I were the lucky ones . to be reporting on the telecast. I remember the salt spray hitting my face as the craft bounced over the white caps to the towering carrier. In a small way, I felt like I was coming home, and I even wore my Navy Reserve ensign uniform.

While preparations were being made, a Navy helicopter came in for a landing on the deck. Klaus's mind worked a mile a minute, and he was always trying to improve the visual possibilities of a telecast. Keep in mind that videotape hadn't been invented yet, so you only could show what was going on at the moment. With so many variables, there was little chance of pre-planning too many of the events. But Klaus was always so flexible, and he seized the chance to try something he had thought about for a long time.

"Commander, what about sending a camera up in the helicopter?"

"I don't know," the officer answered. "We've never done it before. Is it even possible? I thought those cameras were too big for a chopper." He paused and turned to Klaus. "What about the cable?"

"I could feed a lot of cable to the camera if the helicopter went up slowly. It could go higher than the bridge of the carrier and give us a great shot of the action."

The Commander hesitated. "I don't know."

"Who can we check with?" Klaus asked.

Klaus then explained his plan to the Captain, then to his executive officer, then to the helicopter pilot. Everyone liked the idea and agreed that it would be an interesting experiment. After the pilot got further details about weight and size of the cable, and how it would be dangled out of the helicopter, he had no hesitation about trying it. Ed Reznick, our cameraman, was surprised by how easily the camera squeezed into the helicopter. He simply kept it on his lap and shot through the open door.

The holiday broadcast went smoothly, with the fireworks, the interview with the skipper, and the guests visiting the flight decks all going off without a hitch. But the highlight of the evening was the live picture from the helicopter as it rose to about fifty feet above the carrier's deck. The summer of 1953 was the first time that a live picture was televised from a helicopter in flight. It was quite a sight in the darkening sky, hovering over the flight deck with fifty feet of cable hanging out the side door and another hundred feet or so coiled on the deck below.

It made a huge impression on Klaus. The flight test had really only been a stunt to make one telecast more interesting. But Klaus was miles ahead of everyone in thinking that a helicopter would make a magnificent flying television station. The first thing he had to figure out was how to get rid of the dangling cable.

Klaus passed the dream on to one of his chief engineers, John Silva, who was tasked with putting a helicopter into the air with a miniature camera, makeshift transmitting equipment, and a complete broadcasting studio on board. What a challenge! And not only did he succeed, he did it *ten years* before anyone else in the industry. Because of his foresight, KTLA was soon flying its copter before police and fire departments even considered the possibility of having their own. Once again, in the Landsberg tradition, KTLA scooped the nation.

The Loss of Klaus Landsberg

With everything going so right for KTLA, it still feels so wrong that fate took such a cruel detour.

Klaus Landsberg was diagnosed with cancer in 1956, and it was evident he would not last long. He had been very sick for much of that year, and as summer wore on, he had to spend more time away from his beloved KTLA. In spite of his condition, he still operated the station. He watched the air picture closely, read all of the daily reports, and continued to plan for future shows.

It was a difficult time. Klaus was loosening the reins ever so slowly. I worked especially closely with Klaus during that year, and more and more of the station's operation fell to me. In turn, I allowed each department head to take more responsibility. When anything special had to be done, Klaus would ask our sales manager, Bob Mohr, or me to do it.

Klaus's Last Deal

John Polich, a director and engineer who was very close to Klaus, had talked to Barney Clougherty, the owner of the Farmer John Meat Packing Company, about buying time on KTLA. As luck would have it, Barney had just underwritten *Polka Parade*, a musical costume show with plenty of old-world charm and music, the kind of show that appealed to many ethnic groups in Los Angeles. John convinced Barney to put them on KTLA. Although Klaus was very sick, he insisted that John bring Barney up to his Hollywood Hills home to talk about the show. I was invited to join them for lunch.

This was the first time I had seen Klaus in about two weeks, and his weight loss was shocking. Even though Klaus was frail, he was cheerful and determined to close the deal. Barney and Klaus liked each other from the start, and they had a lot in common. The deal was set before lunch was finished,. Barney Clougherty kept *Polka Parade* on KTLA for over fifteen years, fondly remembering his meeting with Klaus, whom he always referred to as "The Dutchman."

It was the final sale Klaus would make.

That lunch meeting at his house was the last time I saw Klaus. He was optimistic and looking forward to the future, determined not to let the cancer beat him. I almost believed he would win. But the fall of 1956 brought Klaus's life to a close.

I had just finished the first part of our *Fisherman's Fiesta* telecast, which was a parade of floral-decorated boats that floated down the main channel of the harbor like a Rose Parade on water. This was an annual telecast that Klaus had always directed, but John Silva filled in that year.

It took me a few minutes to get to the dockside location where our mobile units were. When I walked into the control room before the boat parade began, I could tell something was wrong. John Silva had just been told that Klaus had passed away. It was with heavy hearts that we did the broadcast that Sunday morning.

It was almost impossible to think of KTLA without Klaus. He was its brilliant leader, its driving force and inspiration, and he was the person who made everything work. He was one of the few great men I have ever known.

It was almost as if Klaus knew his time on earth was short, and this made him determined to accomplish so much with the time he had. He left an impressive legacy at KTLA, and we were determined to pick up where he left off. Doing the impossible became commonplace for us, and striving to be the best became second nature. And while he was here, how great those years were! It's hard to look back and remember that it all began on a sound stage on the Paramount lot in the summer of 1942.

Chapter 8
Going Back to the Birth of KTLA with Klaus Landsberg

Today KTLA operates out of a sprawling, ten-acre site in Hollywood that used to belong to Warner Brothers. Historical milestones are all around it. It's only a few blocks from "Gower Gulch," where many of the earliest Hollywood movies were made. In 1927, the first talking feature film was shot here. Al Jolson made the "Jazz Singer," which was a revolutionary development in the history of motion pictures, on stage six. The silver screen began to talk, and the movies were changed forever.

That same year, a little more than a mile from the KTLA station, in his home laboratory on New Hampshire Street, television pioneer Philo Farnsworth made a breakthrough by devising one of the first practical electronic television systems to transmit pictures from one point to another. This meant that the silver screen was moving out of the movie theatre and into the home. Commercial television was about to become a reality. Some called it radio with pictures, or motion pictures in the living room, but in 1947, television was here.

And yet, most people didn't even know it existed. There were few sets to buy in stores, and those who had them were hobbyists who made their receivers from television kits. Television for the masses was still a long way off.

At the time, moviemakers considered television to be something like an exotic toy: an interesting concept that might be fun to play with someday. Since Paramount Pictures had hired a young German scientist named Klaus Landsberg to head up its experimental station, he was the only one who knew anything about television. Studio officials left him alone to operate the station.

A refugee from Hitler's Germany, Klaus was on the engineering team that televised the 1936 Olympic Games in Berlin, and was an engineer with NBC on its history-making telecasts from the New York World's Fair in 1939 that marked the start of television broadcasting in the United States.

In Germany, young Klaus had developed a navigational system using electronic sound. His experiments were in the scientific areas that led to the radar and sonar discoveries during World War II. When his requests for patents on some of his inventions were classified as military secrets by the Nazis, he knew it was time to leave Germany. He arrived in the United States with his inventions in hand, and immediately turned them over to US authorities.

Klaus joined television pioneer Allen B. Dumont and took part in many of his early experimental television projects. Paramount Pictures was an investor in Dumont's laboratory efforts, and when they announced plans to build a television station in Los Angeles, Klaus was picked to be its general manager.

He built the station's transmitter himself. It was the most powerful transmitter at that time, in fact, and he built it using only hard-to-find spare parts. He placed it on a perfect site for transmission—the 6,000-foot peak of Mount Wilson. It provided television coverage to most of Southern California. While all of the other stations eventually followed his lead and set up shop on Mount Wilson, Klaus had the advantage of the sharp, clear picture transmitted by KTLA.

Paramount was a very busy place in the summer of 1942. The war was on and the studio was making pictures as fast as sound stages could be cleared. The make-believe world moved at a brisk pace. Wardrobe people pushed racks to their assigned sets, and costumed actors paced back and forth, balancing cups of coffee while studying their scripts. It wasn't unusual to see a Bobby from London talking to a Japanese soldier from Bataan in front of a stage door.

Dick Lane, an actor on contract with Paramount Studios was walking to the sound stage where his latest film was being made when he passed the studio's old still gallery. He stopped in front of the open door and looked at the new equipment that had replaced the old movie gear.

"What do you have in here?" Dick asked, peeking inside.

A voice with a slight German accent came from the studio. "Some television equipment."

Dick was intrigued. "You mean television works? I thought that was something for the future."

"Well, you're right. We're putting it together for our experimental station."

"I'm Dick Lane," he said, sticking his hand out. "I'm working on the stage next to you."

"I recognized you from all your films, Dick. I'm Klaus Landsberg and this is my station." He pointed to a scattered assembly of unopened boxes, workbenches, and electronic equipment in the old studio.

That was the beginning of a great friendship.

"When you're ready to do some programs, I'd like to help out," Dick said, one of the many times he wandered over to the studio.

Have Station, Need Show

Klaus kept Dick's offer in mind. In September of 1942, Dick Lane became one of the first people to appear on Klaus Landsberg's experimental television station, W6XYZ. He was the master of ceremonies for a musical talent show, *Hits and Bits*. Klaus built a small control room in one section of the stage with a portable console, and he had a single camera set up where film and slides could be projected directly onto it. Two other Dumont Iconoscope cameras stood on the stage, ready for live broadcasts. Klaus had two engineers at the television transmitter on Mount Wilson. The total workforce of the station was six, including Dick Lane, the new emcee.

Hits and Bits and other public service shows were televised over the experimental station during the war years. Most were simple productions that dealt with civil defense, wartime news, and entertainment broadcasts.

Less Civil Defense, More Entertainment

Acting and television were just two of Dick's interests. He was also into professional wrestling, and was Danny McShane's manager.

"How is Danny doing, Dick?" Klaus asked one afternoon when Dick walked into the garage.

Dick beamed. "Won again last night."

"How do you think wrestling would do on television? Do you think the public would go for it?"

Dick was ambivalent. "I don't know. It appeals to a special group."

"It would be easy to televise. We could do it right here."

"Here? But you'd need an arena like the Hollywood Legion or the Olympic Auditorium."

Klaus wasn't going to be dissuaded. "We could start here and see how it goes. If it does well, we'll move to someplace bigger."

"Sure, Klaus, count me in."

Dick Lane began announcing wrestling matches from the garage studios. His enthusiasm and colorful descriptions created instant excitement and helped build wrestling into the first big new sport on television. The matches outgrew the garage and were moved to the Olympic Auditorium in downtown Los Angeles. Attendance surged, and wrestling became a new television sport that appealed to a surprisingly large audience.

Wrestling was good programming for W6XYZ because it was inexpensive to produce, and it filled up a lot of airtime. Wrestling stars like Gorgeous George, Barone Leone, and Lord Blears vied with Dick Lane to become the most recognizable television star.

When KTLA inaugurated commercial television in the West, Dick Lane was the announcer, but the host was Bob Hope. Dick's opening line was: "This distinguished audience is on hand to witness the production of the most ambitious television program yet undertaken. . . . This is Hollywood's first all-star program." Dick Lane ushered in the commercial era of television in January, 1947.

Much of Klaus's programming format was based on the wide appeal of popular live music. It was universal entertainment and he capitalized on it with shows like *Dixie Showboat*—which had Dick Lane as the sideburned Mississippi riverboat captain and emcee—Ina Ray Hutton and her orchestra, *Hollywood Opportunity, Harry Owens and his Royal Hawaiians,* and four shows with Lawrence Welk and his band.

As good as Klaus was, he wasn't always right. He didn't think Jackie Gleason was funny and predicted he would never make it on television. Klaus also turned down a show featuring Liberace, who went on to become one of the big stars on television.

But for every time he struck out, Klaus hit at least three out of the ballpark, and did it with style and ingenuity. As an example, Klaus wanted to schedule a western action film every afternoon because the station had a large library of them. On their own, many weren't very good, but packaged together they could appeal to a large audience. Klaus had it all figured out: there would be a little western set that included a fence post, bunk house, a wagon wheel or two, a background with open fields painted on it, and some children who would be invited onto the show each day. The last detail was finding a cowboy to host the program.

With so many cowboys in Hollywood, Klaus had a sizeable list to of possible candidates. Problem was, he was on a time crunch. He looked no further than his creative art director, Sherman Laudermilk.

"Sherm, why don't you go over to wardrobe and get yourself a cowboy outfit? You would be an excellent host."

Sherman thought Klaus was kidding.

"You could do it in the afternoon, and it wouldn't interfere with any of your regular art work on other programs." He sat forward and smiled at Sherman. "We can call you Cowboy Slim."

Cowboy Slim became the star of the program. In typical KTLA fashion, Sherm simply added the assignment to his regular work schedule. The program caught on and Cowboy Slim became one of the most popular hosts of children's programs on television. He was so successful that another local station offered him a similar spot at double the money. He accepted, and KTLA lost not only a popular children's television personality, but also a great art director.

Announcer Tom Hatten did double duty as a cartoonist, so Klaus put Tom in a sailor's cap, set up his drawing easel, and had him host a series of *Popeye* cartoons. Its immense popularity was the perfect lead-in to the news program.

Frank Herman became an important part of KTLA when he came on board as Skipper Frank on *Cartoon Carousel* at 5:00 p.m. every weekday. These cartoon hosts became great role models for children watching television through those years, and hundreds of kids would show up on weekends at local shopping malls and business centers when the television hosts made personal appearances.

It was ironic that the demise of the hosts on children's shows resulted from those who objected to the commercials on the programs. Since the hosts did many commercials, a vocal minority believed they were taking unfair advantage of the kids, forcing unwanted products on them. Gradually the opposition grew, and the hosts disappeared from the screen. That exciting era of children's shows that so many people fondly remembered came to an early end. It was doubly ironic that the hosts disappeared but the commercials remained.

But Klaus never allowed adversity to prevail. He was always willing to try something new, and most of all he believed in the news. If a big news story developed, programs and commercials were cancelled and he'd make sure that the event was covered. This live breakthrough coverage made a big impression on viewers because they became a part of the action. It riveted our attention, it intruded on our lives, it upset us, it made a mark on us.

That was all due to Klaus Landsberg, who in his short lifetime pioneered much of what we consider the best in television today.

CHAPTER 9

The Telecopter: Our Best-Kept Secret

In 1957, the idea of having helicopters that could carry live electronic cameras and operate as a flying television station was of little interest to the industry. Equipment was too bulky and the cost of developing a smaller, lightweight camera that could transmit good quality pictures was enormous. But in those early years, KTLA's chief engineer John Silva didn't worry about what couldn't be done. He concentrated on making the impossible happen.

General Manager Jim Schulke gave Silva the go-ahead to build the first Telecopter. Silva was concerned that other network stations with bigger budgets and unlimited equipment could beat us at our own game, but since his experimental lab was away from the station, he could work in a complete vacuum from the rest of the industry. He had to use primitive equipment to somehow develop a flying television station.

He began with two main problems: weight and space. John estimated that the copter would have to carry about two thousand pounds of electronic equipment, and there was no way he could cram all of that gear aboard and still make the copter flyable. He immediately set his sights on getting a bigger copter that could carry more weight, but he hit a budgetary snag. In addition, the larger size would be impractical for daily use over populated areas where news stories were likely to take place.

The smaller Bell helicopter was the most-used model at the time. It could carry a pilot and a passenger, plus a payload of about four hundred pounds. The problem was that to meet that four hundred pound limit, the copter could carry only half of its normal fuel supply. This would restrict it from long flights, but it would give the station great coverage over the city.

John then turned to the problem of squeezing two thousand pounds of equipment into four hundred airborne pounds. He worked on existing parts and electronic equipment, redesigning, reshaping, and cutting out everything he could. He had an industry pipeline to what changes could be expected in the near future, and he depended on those to save him hundreds of pounds. When he found the new items he needed, he made deals with the companies to use their products and give them field testing. It was a beneficial for everyone—John got to use the new generations of electronic equipment, and when the products were ready for the market, the manufacturers could say they had already been thoroughly tested by KTLA.

With all the dramatic changes on the horizon, Silva designed his helicopter at the right time. Transistors were a particularly great development because those miniaturized components went into his transmitting gear and helped reduce weight. But even with all the new advances, space inside the bubble of the copter was still too cramped, so John added boxes on top of the landing skids to carry extra gear.

He had a big problem selecting the right antenna for the copter. After numerous experiments, he decided on the General Electric helical antenna, which was made for UHF television stations, but it was too big for the copter. John had reached a dead end.

He broke his self-imposed secrecy to tell GE engineers about his problem. The technicians studied his specifications at the GE plant in Syracuse, New York, and they were able to modify the antenna design into a smaller, efficient, and workable unit. The actual antenna was put together in the Paramount Studio workshop.

To complete the secrecy of the operation, a Bell helicopter was hauled from the Van Nuys hangar to Dick Hart's Studio City garage, where the miniaturized equipment was installed under the guidance of Silva and Hart. And with that, Silva had actually done it. He'd shrunk the original two thousand pounds of equipment down to 368 pounds by the time the craft finally received its CAA government approval.

Dick Hart hauled the craft back to Van Nuys Airport, where it was ready to be flown. Hart took it on its first test flight on July 3, 1958. The flight went beautifully. The next day, pilot Bob Gilbreath took the Telecopter up with John, doing double duty as cameraman-engineer. His pictures were shot out the window and transmitted to Mount Wilson. The Telecopter was a reality.

After a year of secrecy and rumors, KTLA's flying television station took its first flight in front of a stunned industry, making pilot-reporter Larry Scheer and cameraman-engineer Harold Morby the very first people in the world to transmit the news from a helicopter.

There were lots of developments to the copter over the years. Equipment got better, cameras got smaller, and the black and white pictures changed to color. The small Bell was replaced by another model, and eventually the Telecopter became a Jet Ranger. The Telecopter became the envy of every news department across the country, and it was many years before anyone was able to match it. The copter gave KTLA its exclusive edge in covering all the major stories for many years to come.

I recall one of the first news assignments for the new Telecopter involved covering the circus that was coming to town. As part of the hoopla surrounding the arrival, ten elephants were scheduled to parade down Hollywood Boulevard, and the copter was sent up to show pictures of them marching trunk-in-tail through the city. However, the story was a scrub. Although there were supposedly ten elephants down there, the Telecopter couldn't find them!

Our News Director Gil Martyn muttered, "How do you like that, ten elephants in the middle of Hollywood Boulevard, and you can't even find one of them with the Telecopter."

The Telecopter did much better on subsequent stories, thanks to the talents of pilot-reporter Larry Scheer. Larry was an experienced helicopter pilot who could multitask with the best. I was often in the newsroom relaying information to him over the radio while he was broadcasting on the air. He'd just weave the new facts into his narration and continue to report the story. Larry could give you a concise, sixty-second report or he could continue reporting for long periods of time, depending on the requirements of the news coverage.

He was a superb, cautious pilot and could handle any emergency situation. He refused to do anything foolhardy or dangerous, but he always came back with the story.

The Telecopter flew from 1958 to 1973. For fifteen years it covered news from the skies of Los Angeles. Of course, helicopters are an accepted part of television news coverage today, but it took years before other stations started using a copter like the one at KTLA. Even today, none of the latest models have been able to duplicate the live picture quality we had.

In 1973, KTLA changed its emphasis on news and sold the Telecopter to KNBC, Los Angeles. Larry Scheer left the station to continue flying the Telecopter for KNBC. Larry was later succeeded by Francis Gary Powers, the famous U-2 pilot shot down over the Soviet Union in 1960. In a sad footnote, Powers and a KNBC engineer were flying back from covering a brush fire near Santa Barbara when the Telecopter encountered engine trouble and crashed in a field not far from Van Nuys airport. Both Powers and his passenger were killed.

CHAPTER 10

The Fractured Fifties: Down From the Up Side

Pages are turned so often in life. Some bring minor reversals while others radically change your direction. A big chapter closed for me in September of 1958, with the death of my mentor and former program director, Gordon Wright, from cancer. Gordon gave me my first job in television, and I owe him so much. He'd left the station years before and, as often happens in this business, we had drifted apart. I didn't know how sick he was, and his death came as a great shock.

Everyone has a personal story about how they got started in television. It's usually the accidental blend of circumstances that results in an offer. Gordon had had a lot of airtime he was responsible for filling, and decided that my out-of-the-blue phone call was a prophetic sign. He was impressed with my recent graduation from USC, and decided to give me a chance. Under his tutelage, I learned how to withstand crisis and pressure, since he was a master at it and could wade through the most terrifying of incidents with ease. I copied his calm approach, and it's an adopted trait that has served me well for sixty years.

Another one of those accidental blends of circumstances in my early years came by way of Gil Martyn, KTLA's news director. I was in the sales department and was interested in getting involved with the news. In essence, I was an outsider, not a newsman who worked in the field. But Gil knew of my interest and accepted me as part of his operation. He always gave me support and encouragement along the way, even though I remained an outsider for a while longer.

When doctors found Gil's throat cancer, they insisted an operation was essential. The surgery impaired his voice and left visible scars that needed time to heal. In the interim, I anchored his 6:30 news broadcast. It was a busy and exciting time, since I hadn't given up my day job in sales. The temporary job as a newscaster lasted fifteen months, and Gil was very helpful during that time. As the months wore on, it became apparent that he would be unable to return to his anchor position. He did a few stories, but he knew that his days as an on-air reporter were over.

Gil died a few months later. His death came far too close to Klaus's death two years earlier. How could it be that three of my closest friends had been hit by the same cruel disease? Those three men had been instrumental in helping me develop a career in television, and I took their passing very hard.

The station held off a long time before announcing that a new anchorman would take Gil's place. They were able to bridge the time by keeping me on the air as Gil's temporary replacement.

A Brief Stint on the Air Invites Other Possibilities

I enjoyed the nightly newscast; it was what I'd always wanted to do. It was my great fortune to have had the opportunity to do so at KTLA instead of having to leave town and settle in some other city. When the word came down that I was to be taken off the program, I was crushed. I'd had the chance to make it and fell short. I was good enough to be Gil's temporary replacement, but not good enough to be a permanent newscaster. It hurt like none other.

My goal was to spend all my television years in news and special events. After reaching that goal, I ached at having to give it up. I kept the morning and daytime news broadcasts, and I was still used on special news events as they happened. So instead of feeling completely dejected and discouraged, I solidified my long-range goals and decided to view this new arrangement as only a transition to a new opportunity.

That outlook was fueled by the rumors floating around that soon I would have the chance to move out of the sales department and become a full-time announcer. I was elated at the possibility. I'd done the other jobs because they were essential and had to be done.

They were the work. The on-the-air spots were the fun. Somehow the two had to be blended together. As long as I had some chance to be on camera, I was willing to work long and hard at the other jobs.

I'll admit that the prospect of being on camera full-time also brought along a host of concerns; the main one being that I was would be forced to limit my options. As it had been, if my on-air work didn't pan out, I always had the sales department to fall back on. If sales took a dip, I had my camera work to back it up. It was a good combination, in spite of the long hours, and I looked at it as the price to be paid for having the double opportunity. The high sales commission checks were great for a man with a growing family, but I knew didn't want to give up my on-air work.

I had always remained silent about my personal preference because the new executives at the station didn't know me that well. In my ten years at the station, I'd been at the center of the operation. Now, in the fall of 1958, I was being given more limited duties. It was difficult to watch my personal center-stage action of the past ten years slip away. Now others were beginning run the station, and I would become just an announcer, a reporter, or whatever else I was assigned to do.

The unsettling events in my television career seemed to mirror changes going on all around me. The worldview of the 1950s began unraveling with the Korean War, and the effects of its disintegration were beginning to show.

Many of the Korean War veterans experienced homecomings similar to those the Vietnam veterans would have two decades later. They were not welcomed home with open arms and parades. Their war was on hostile Asian soil and never really ended. There was no decisive victory, but a whimpering stalemate.

Some of these vets had fought two wars in five years and were awfully disillusioned with the so-called American Dream. They were turned off by the mad dash for prosperity and material things. They hated conformity and were repulsed by those in the mainstream rat race. They wanted to be different and, in their personal revolt, they set up a new conformity of their own. They could be seen on the beaches at Venice, in the new-style coffeehouses, and in small clusters on college campuses. They wore butch haircuts, old sweat shirts, and khaki pants. Many wore sandals and sported beards. These were the symbols of their disdain for the system that had alienated them. They were no longer fighting it. They were merely dropping out.

Popular music caught the changing tides of the fifties. Chubby Checker did a dance called the Twist. Bill Haley and the Comets sang "Rock Around the Clock" and Elvis Presley crashed onto the music scene. The contemporary music world would never be the same.

Few of our news broadcasts reflected many of these rumbling changes because life, for the majority of the country, stayed on an even keel. It was ironic that at a time when the world seemed almost controllable, a big gash ripped open its stability with the civil rights movement, and "We Shall Overcome" became a call heard in every state.

In the early sixties we decided to produce an hour special about what high school students worried about in their day-to-day life. We sent our huge mobile units out to a youth camp in Malibu for an all-day conference with student leaders in an effort to learn about the big problems on campus. These were the best and the brightest; student body officers came from schools all over the city to take part in discussing problems facing their friends on campus. School officials hoped they might find some answers to these problems.

When our broadcast went on the air, the "big issues" turned out to be pretty minor. We listened as student leaders talked about the problems of keeping the campus clean, about devising ways to cut down on talking in the classrooms, how to get better behavior in the hallways, what should be done about smoking on campus, and students who wore clothes that were too extreme for school.

That's not too bad when you consider that today's high school discussions would most certainly deal with drugs, alcohol, teen pregnancies, gang warfare, assaults on teachers, campus fights, and robberies. How things have changed.

The Impact of Clete Roberts

Shifting social tides were gathering force as the fifties gave way to the sixties. Clete Roberts was the reporter who would bridge the sudden social changes for the station. He was already well known in the industry, and he brought a faithful audience with him when he moved to KTLA. He quickly established himself as the station's anchorman and became one of the most-watched newsmen on the air.

Since Clete was best known as a foreign correspondent who reported from international trouble spots, he modernized KTLA news by developing his own network of cameramen in major cities around the world. They would send him film whenever breaking news stories occurred in their countries, and he'd report it on the air in California.

His foreign correspondent image was reinforced every night when his newscast opened with shots of him in his trench coat, passport in hand, stepping off an airplane. He was the perfect example of what viewers thought a foreign correspondent should look like. His image enhanced the station's news coverage reputation and increased our audience.

Clete used his network of cameras to take the audience to where things were happening, and it was during his years at KTLA that the picture took center stage. His personal experiences with international news brought a sophisticated flavor to his nightly commentaries since he had observed many of them firsthand.

He was just as effective on the local scene. During a breaking story, Clete knew how to get the most from the live camera. When a devastating fire hit the mountains of Bel Air in 1961, Clete and his team of reporters presented one of the most powerful and dramatic telecasts ever seen. This was also the first telecast for the KTLA Telecopter, and the power of those visuals brought the fire's devastating effects to millions of viewers in Los Angeles and across the country.

The copter was in the air and Clete was right there on the ground, where the flames were consuming homes on both sides of the street. During the long broadcast, the new Telecopter captured the magnitude of the erratic path of the rolling red ball of flames as it devoured almost everything on the mountain range. It was powerful television, and I was fortunate enough to have been one of the reporters working with Clete and Bill Stout on that telecast.

Clete was asked to take over the entire news operation when he came to KTLA from CBS in 1959. He brought in his own news company to produce the broadcasts, and was responsible for hiring the first television news film cameramen, sound men, and film editors at KTLA. Prior to Roberts, there were none.

The news operation was small but effective, and Clete's broadcasts soon became one of the highest-rated news programs on the air. It ran for thirty minutes and featured a sports segment with the former Michigan All American football star, Tom Harmon, one of the best-known television sportscasters at the time. Clete also had a special news segment with reporter Pat Michaels and later Tom Franklin. The combination worked very well and "The Big Three" dominated the news.

With Clete's handprint on our nightly news, international events were making a big impact at KTLA. It had been announced that Premier Khrushchev was making his first trip to America in 1959, so I went to the Soviet Union to film a documentary about life in Moscow. My trip would have never been possible if not for Khrushchev's relaxed position on allowing foreign reporters into the Soviet Union, and I was thrilled to be a part of one of the first foreign crews to venture into Russia. But it wasn't going to be easy. To begin with, we didn't have anything close to the level of sophistication of today's equipment. To record the trip, Clete loaned me his handheld Bell and Howell camera, and I shot about 2,500 feet of black and white film of the people of Moscow and the amazing scenery. My documentary was shown on KTLA when Premier Khrushchev visited Los Angeles that fall.

The station received the coveted Peabody Award for our extended coverage of Khrushchev's historic trip to Los Angeles. We were even fortunate enough to have snared an exclusive interview with Khrushchev at the L.A. train station at the very end of his whirlwind tour of Los Angeles. We had our cameras set up, my questions were prepared, and all we needed was for Khrushchev to appear for our half-hour exclusive.

His limo arrived and we waited. And waited. Word came down that he was refusing to get out of the car because he was still furious over remarks made at a public ceremony with L.A. Mayor Poulson, who took exception to Khrushchev's continued touting of Russian superiority during his tour. Bringing up Khrushchev's infamous comment, "We will bury you," Poulson responded, "You shall not bury us and we shall not bury you. We tell you in the friendliest terms possible we are planning no funerals, yours or our own."

Even though Poulson received over 3,600 letters of approval following the incident, I watched my interview with Khrushchev melt away because he refused to get out of the car. There I was, stuck on the air, talking for a half hour to fill up the time. News is fluid and unpredictable and, sometimes, so are the interviewees.

Stepping in to Take Up the Slack

When the *Daily Mirror*, owned by the *Los Angeles Times*, folded in 1960, Clete believed television news should step in to fill the void, and he assigned me to anchor a morning newscast. Larry Tighe, Julian Wolinsky, and I produced the half-hour show each morning, five days a week, for more than a year. After the newscast, I became the staff announcer, and did several five-minute newscasts throughout the day.

KTLA was riding high and, as can happen when you're at the top, became a target to be bettered. Channel 2 was working on a new format that would set the pattern for all future news operations. It was called *The Big News*, and it featured Jerry Dunphy, Maury Green, Ralph Storey, Saul Halpert, and Bill Keane. It was an unprecedented one-hour broadcast filled with excellent news film pieces and a wide range of stories. It cut into the big ratings that Clete had built up, and went on to dominate the local news scene in Los Angeles for years.

When Clete left the station, my daytime newscasts were again cut back and I was not included in the station's expanded news operation. I was on the fringe of news once again and not a part of the new emphasis. After nearly fifteen years in the business, I'd learned to roll with the punches and not get discouraged over the setbacks. Instead, I became involved in many non-news activities, but I held out hope that one day I might again be an active member of the newsroom operation.

Now, instead of news, I found myself involved in game shows.

CHAPTER 11

Game Shows , then Back to the News

Early in the sixties, KTLA aced out its competitors by airing game shows during prime time. These audience-participation programs had been a mainstay of the networks during daytime hours, but our program director, Bob Quinlan, believed that the 7:00 to 8:00 p.m. time slot was wide open, just waiting for a station that was willing to try something new. All three of the networks were broadcasting their national news programs from 7:00 to 7:30, followed with a local program at 7:30. Since there were no major entertainment shows on the air during this hour, Bob decided it was a perfect time for some creative counter-programming.

At first, the station televised the new game shows live every night, until the new videotape machines began replacing film projectors in master control. Videotape revolutionized the industry, and the producers took advantage of its cost-effective benefits. Now one production crew could videotape three shows in their eight-hour shift, and the programs could be syndicated to other stations around the country.

It was during this time that KTLA made me the announcer on some of the game shows. It was a good break for me, and I worked the game shows after my regular announcing shift. Even though I basically had two jobs, I also got two paychecks. During the day I was a staff announcer and did about a half dozen *Telecopter News* broadcasts, then in the evenings I'd hop over to another stage on the lot and do my stint as a game show announcer.

I was the off-camera voice at the start of the show, and it was my job to announce the prizes the contestants were trying to win. What could have been easier? Well, I soon realized that my most important job was trying to keep the studio audience happy before the show started, which was no small task. For one thing, it wasn't easy back then to gather an audience for the shows, so the station had to hire someone who specialized in collecting people. She brought them to KTLA, let them stand in line for a while, then delivered them to the studio when we were ready to tape the program.

When we were doing the live shows, everything ran like clockwork. I'd welcome the audience, make them feel at home, tell a few jokes, and introduce them to the host. I had my earphones on to get the cues, a bright light over my script, a microphone stand at the side of the stage, and I read my copy when the director cued me. It was an easy formula that I followed every night.

However, things started to change when we began videotaping the shows. The new tape machines were always breaking down, and that could mean a ten or fifteen minute wait while the engineers opened up the new machines and tried to troubleshoot the problem. The cast and crew would just go backstage, run through their scripts, have a cup of coffee, and wait until the engineers were ready to go again.

It was a very different story for me. I had a hundred or so people sitting in the audience, growing restless. I had already done my spiel before the show started. Now I was out of steam and caught in the position of having to fill a void while the equipment was being fixed. Since it was my job to keep the audience relaxed and happy until the show began again, I had to do a lot of improvising.

I'd trained for a lot of jobs, but I had no track record as a stand-up comedian. Initially, I talked to the audience, explaining that the tape machine had broken, then went on to tell a few stories about the shows and answer any questions they had. That worked for a little while, but not for extended periods of time.

My saving grace was a recently completed memory course with famed memory expert Arthur Bornstein. I began making it a point to be at the door when the audience first came into the theatre. I'd shake hands and get to know them on a one-on-one basis before the official warm-up. The questions I asked were standard: where they were from, their occupation, that sort of thing. Then, when the tape machine broke down, I'd go down to the audience floor and walk up and down the aisle, talking about each guest personally. They always got a real kick out of how much I remembered about them. This was a perfect solution because I could use as much or as little time as I needed. Like an accordion, I could squeeze the memory act into a couple of minutes or stretch it out to a half hour—however long it took for the technical snafus to be corrected.

"Now, Jane, John, Paul, Mrs. Webster, Anne, Harry, and Rachael," I said, while walking up the aisle and looking at each of them in turn. "We met before the show, so of course I remember all of your names. But in my memory course, they taught me that I could meet twenty, thirty, even forty people and remember their names. Should I try?"

On a good night I could remember the names of as many as fifty people in the audience. It made a good impression on everyone, and, more importantly, it filled up a lot of time. The memory routine ended up being better than a standard comedy routine would have been, and it kept the audience in the right mood for the broadcast. The technique ended up being so successful that we never did an official warm up again.

Those were long, busy days for me. My announcing shift started before eight in the morning, I did my live newscasts and worked in the announcer's booth until about five, then I would usually go home for a quick nap before going back to the station for the game shows. Sometimes I woke up in total darkness, not knowing what time it was, not sure whether I was going to work for my morning news shift or going back at night for my game shows.

In those years, KTLA ran movies in the morning. My on-air announcing was limited to the sign-on, a few public service announcements, an occasional station break, and a rare tag to a film commercial. From 8:00 until 11:30 in the mornings, I sat and read the newspaper or a book in the announcer's booth, waiting for the next announcement. At one point, I decided I was wasting too much time and decided to do some writing. I brought my portable typewriter and went to work writing a book. I spent a couple of hours on it each day and wrote almost a thousand pages before I put it in a desk at home, where it has been ever since.

By noon, I would begin getting ready for my newscasts. They were different from any other news program on the air because we had the Telecopter up in the air, ready to catch any breaking story. Even if there was no major event taking place, the Telecopter showed scenes and events from all over Los Angeles. As the reporter on *Telecopter News*, people often assumed I was the copter pilot. In truth, Larry Scheer, Harold Morby, and Matt Zadroga were the airship crew. I was just the announcer at the studio and, in fact, was in our Telecopter only once. Between the assumption of being a pilot on the *Telecopter News* and as talented a memory expert as Authur Bornstein on the game shows, I was flying under false colors; flattering but untrue.

My informal memory routine on the game shows ended when a new network producer from New York took over and decided that studio announcers should warm up the audience from the stage, not from the aisles. My new assignment was to tell jokes and get the audience laughing. It was difficult, but I tried my best. Fortunately, by the time that producer arrived, the tape machines didn't break down as often.

The informal nature of warming up the audience wasn't the only thing that changed around that time. Jack Barry, Tom Kennedy, Jack Narz, Dennis James, and Mike Stokey, the successful, well-known personalities that hosted the different game shows, moved on to network programs. It wasn't long before I was the senior man on the shows.

Just Call Me KTLA's Best Infielder

In the summer of 1963, I decided that I had to do something about my throat. I was always hoarse and frequently sick. The doctors said that I needed to have my tonsils out, so I took a week's vacation and had it done. While I was still in the hospital, I got a call from Bill Derman, one of the game show producers. Bill had always been a good friend and had used me as the host on several pilot game shows that had never made it to the air. He was calling to ask me to be the new host of KTLA's biggest game show. My throat was so sore that I couldn't even whisper a "thank you" on the phone, and Beverly had to do the talking. Unfortunately, he needed the new host to start the next night. There was nothing to be done. Beverly thanked him, and someone else got the job. Not too long after that, my days with game shows came to an end.

My employment with KTLA was like being a utility infielder on a baseball team. The managers needed dependable and talented backup, in case of any emergencies, and it got so I could play any position. I was the announcer who appeared with the *Los Angeles Times* society editor on one of the big social events of the year, The Las Floristas Headdress Ball. I announced the Rose Parade with the garden and flower editor of the *Sunday Magazine*. I teamed up with a horseracing expert to broadcast the weekly quarter horse race from Los Alamitos. When Dick Lane was on vacation, I announced the speedboat races from then-little-known Lake Los Angeles, which is now the huge Marina Del Rey harbor complex. When Larry Finley was sick, I did his overnight talk show from a Long Beach nightclub, interviewing celebrities and introducing musical acts until the early hours of the morning. When Paul Langford was away for a few months, I did his Sunday morning real estate show. It ran for more than an hour and I showed pictures of new housing developments and discussed the latest news in real estate.

On occasion, when the hostess of *Romper Room* was sick or late, I stepped in and did her hour-long show with a dozen or so preschool children. I had seen the program enough times to follow the general format. One time, as I was leading the kids through the Pledge of Allegiance, I managed to flub it. One of the little girls looked up, corrected me, and led the rest of the children through the remainder of the Pledge. How could it be that I got all the big, important events perfect, and yet managed to mess up the Pledge?

I enjoyed my position as the ultimate utility infielder. It was good to know that our new program director, Bob Quinlan, and his assistant, Loring d'Usseau, would always turn to me when there was something unusual to do. I liked being a jack-of-all-trades.

No Longer the Utility Infielder

A major turning point in my career came in 1963. Even though I was always busy, I had started to feel like I was drifting. For the first time in my life, I was concerned about where I was going in television. Rather than moving closer to the news operation, where I really wanted to be, I seemed to be moving farther away. New people were brought in, yet there didn't appear to be a full-time position for me in the news. I kept telling myself that by doing all of the daytime newscasts, I was still part of the team.

Bob Quinlan was in the process of rebuilding the news department, and one of his moves was to hire Sam Zelman away from KNXT, the local CBS station. Sam was the power behind KNXT's *Big News*, which had dominated the local news scene for years.

Sam Zelman had extensive contacts in the news business, and he was able to search out and sign people he considered to be the best newscasters around the country. He already had Bill Stout, another former CBS newsman and probably the most respected reporter in Los Angeles, at the station. Then he brought in Joe Benti, who later became a well-known CBS anchorman, Tom Snyder, who gained national prominence as a talk show host and newsman, and Bob Arthur, the mainstay of the *Ken and Bob Show* on KABC radio in Los Angeles. Sam also gave CBS reporter Terry Drinkwater his start in television. He hired more camera crews, put together a top news team, and produced an excellent broadcast in no time.

As the daytime newsman, I worked closely with Sam's newly hired news team. I'll admit that it was difficult to see this great news operation being built and not be a part of it. I did the newscasts whenever there was no one else around to do them, and I was assigned to the special live news events when they happened. I wondered if it would always be this way.

The only thing certain in this business is change, and I was determined to stay with it through the ups and downs. Sam knew it could take time to build an audience, but he was sure this combination of proven professionals would be able to start at the top and stay there. Even though Sam Zelman was pleased with the quality of the news, he was disappointed that the newscast didn't take a big jump in ratings right from the start. When it didn't happen right away, he left and returned to CBS. His parting was friendly, and Bob Quinlan asked Sam who he thought should take over the department on a temporary basis.

Sam's reply was quick and decisive: "Stan Chambers."

I became news director on December 1, 1963. Two weeks later I was immersed in my first big story in my new role—the collapse of the Baldwin Hills Dam.

CHAPTER 12
My New Position – Baptism by Fire

The Assassination of President Kennedy

November 22, 1963, is a date that few will ever forget. I was in the newsroom preparing one of my daytime newscasts when I heard the ominous, staccato ringing of the bulletin bell from the UPI newswires. It was one of the few times in my life that I heard a UPI 15-bell flash, and I jumped up from my typewriter and raced to the bank of chattering teletypes. The urgent sound of the chilling bells was accompanied by the word FLASH printed on the Teletype paper. I stared at the wire machine in disbelief. FLASH was followed by two lines: PRESIDENT JOHN F. KENNEDY WAS SHOT IN DALLAS, TEXAS...

In moments I was in front of a television camera, reporting the shooting. I only had a few lines of wire copy in my hand and had to keep on talking. We knew the President had been rushed to a hospital, we knew that he had been wounded, but we didn't know how badly.

While I talked into the camera, my personal thoughts couldn't help but slide to the forefront. In our time and our country, presidents are not assassinated. Certainly that had happened in the days of McKinley, Garfield, and Lincoln, but no longer. The idea that President Kennedy might die from an assassin's bullet was impossible to even consider, let alone mention, as I spoke on the air.

I continued the broadcast for about twenty minutes, ad-libbing around the small amount of information I had from the United Press teletypes, when I was told by someone off-camera that President Kennedy had died. Stunned, I stalled for a moment, staring dumbly at the newsman standing off camera. *Can I say this?* I asked myself. *What if it is not true?* Taking a deep breath, I found my voice and spoke to the newsman. "Are you certain?"

He handed me the wire copy and I read it out loud. "President Kennedy has just died from his gunshot wounds."

I kept talking for another five minutes or so as a few more details came across the teletypes. Then, in a completely unprecedented act of cooperation, the television networks permitted us to join them in their coverage of the assassination. I concluded my part, and KTLA picked up the network feed. The television coverage of the assassination went on for days. It was one of those rare times when every television station in the country broadcasted the same story. The media was mourning along with the nation over the death of its young President.

I was only a small participant in that momentous time, but it was an experience that will always be with me. Many consider this a defining event in American history, after which things would never be the same again. The death of President Kennedy spilled over into everyone's lives. That event seemed to be the dividing line between the old world of the fifties and the turbulent times that followed.

The Dam Collapses

On a Saturday afternoon in early December of 1963, Beverly and I were doing some of our Christmas shopping near the KTLA studios. We were standing in the checkout line when a lady in front of us turned and recognized me. "You're Stan Chambers of KTLA, aren't you?"

"Yes," I answered. "Pleased to meet you."

Her smile turned to a frown. "What are you doing here? The dam is about to break."

I was puzzled. "What dam?"

"The Baldwin Hills Dam. Haven't you heard?"

We'd been shopping for several hours, and I had no way of knowing that a major news event was taking place. Those were the days before pocket beepers and private radios, so it had been impossible for the station to get hold of me. I thanked the woman and quickly walked over to the bank of phones at the other end of the store. Even though I'd lived in Los Angeles all my life, I didn't even know there *was* a dam in Baldwin Hills. I dialed the hotline to the KTLA News Department.

"Stan, we've been trying to get you," they told me. "There's a dam about to go. The Telecopter is already up, and we've called in a crew for the Telemobile. Can you get to the station right away?"

"It'll take me five minutes." I hung up and ran back to Beverly, who was still standing in line. I thanked the woman for the tip, grabbed Beverly, and ran out the store. So much for Christmas shopping.

I felt a hot surge of adrenaline course through my body as we ran to our car. I had been news director for only two weeks and I was missing my first big story! Fortunately Joel Tator, who directed our newscasts, had gotten the word early and raced to the station, where he'd called out all the crews he could find and sent them to the dam site. By the time I got there, everything was going smoothly; our helicopter was being prepped for the flight to the dam and the Telemobile was working its way up the winding road, past the many street blockades.

Police decided to evacuate everyone below the dam, so Joel made arrangements with the program department to periodically cut in on the movies being shown so KTLA could broadcast bulletins telling people to get out.

From the moment I entered the newsroom, I started to gather up as much information as possible. Cracks in the Baldwin Hills Dam had been detected earlier in the day, and water was running out of the walls. While officials publicly said they would be able to handle the situation, the cracks got bigger as the day wore on, and there was a real concern that the whole thing might collapse.

Terry Drinkwater was the reporter with the Telemobile. The crew drove it through the police lines and up the crowded streets, which were filled with residents fleeing the hills around the dam. The evacuation made it extremely difficult to get up those narrow winding streets. Although no one on the crew was familiar with Baldwin Hills, friendly police officers and firemen helped them get to a vacant lot on a bluff on the west side of the dam. It was high enough above the water that it would sustain no damage if the dam failed, but close enough to have a panoramic view of everything. Of course, there was the danger that the entire bluff could be washed away, but the crew seemed comfortable at their spot. They were set and ready to go before anything major occurred.

We still hadn't been able to get a crew for the Telecopter. This was Saturday, and most people were off duty. Harold Morby, our Telecopter cameraman and engineer, was nowhere to be found despite countless phone calls to his home. His back-up cameraman, Matt Zadroga, also had the day off and couldn't be found— probably off Christmas shopping like I had been.

This was one of our vulnerable areas. Since KTLA didn't do any newscasts over the weekend, we gave our crews those days off. When a major event happened on a Saturday, we had to rely on luck. It was a classic example of trying to do everything with a small staff. You can take care of the regular things, but when the unexpected happens, there is a good chance that you may fall flat on your face.

Lou Wolfe, one of our chief engineers who had flown camera in the copter many times, was at home when the phone rang. He raced to the airport so he could be the flying cameraman in the Telecopter. It became a day he would never forget. Don Sides was our new copter pilot, hired for his flying and reporting talents.

Both of them had been thrown into the middle of one of the biggest stories of the decade. They got to the airport and were able to fly to Baldwin Hills before anything major happened. Thanks to Joel Tator's quick thinking and getting news teams out to the dam, I was a lucky news director. We got to the scene on time.

The scene was ominously calm. I was in the studio booth looking at a screen in front of me that showed the picture Don was broadcasting from the copter.

I kept on reporting all of the facts coming into the newsroom. I was talking on the air as the Telecopter showed the pictures of water leaking from the dam. At one point, I was able to get Bob Lee, press officer for the Department of Water and Power, on the telephone, and we interviewed him live. "We're trying to reduce the water level to take the pressure off the dam," Bob said. "We're taking out water as fast as we can."

As he spoke, the copter camera showed a close-up of water pouring through the escape system.

"Mr. Lee, is there any imminent danger that the dam will fail?" I asked, watching the live picture from the Telecopter.

His answer was decisive. "It has held so far, and we believe it will continue to hold—"

At that moment, a circle of concrete fell away from the face of the dam and water came roaring through. I quickly threw the audio to Don Sides in the copter.

Don picked it up. "Just as Bob was talking about the dam holding, it gave way."

He looked down on the unbelievable scene. As more of the dam broke away, water exploded over the catch-basin below, down the winding roads, through the narrow streets, wiping out everything in its path.

The live picture from the Telemobile was terrifying. A huge section of the dam's front disintegrated as the unleashed force of the water kept tearing it away. The floodwater scooped up dozens of automobiles and pushed them down the streets like half-submerged toys. The cars were tossed against houses and buildings which quickly collapsed, and the entire flotsam raced downstream. The worst part about reporting this tragedy was not knowing what happened to the people who lived in those now-shattered homes.

I received calls from networks and television stations all over the country asking for permission to televise our live pictures of the devastation. All the national television networks picked up KTLA's coverage, as the Telecopter overhead and the Telemobile on the ground delivered images that would live in the hearts and minds of many for years to come.

In all, eighty million gallons of water inundated the canyons below the dam and washed out 40,000 tons of debris. More than a hundred homes and apartments were destroyed or badly damaged.

The only positive aspect to this tragedy was that, due to the earlier evacuation order, there were few fatalities.

The Baldwin Hills Dam was never rebuilt. It stood for years, an empty, brush-covered ghost with a large "V" cut out of what used to be the face of the reservoir. It eventually became a city park with rolling lawns and trees, erasing all signs of the devastation and horror. But that December Saturday was etched in the memories of the nation and remains one of Los Angeles' biggest tragedies.

As horrifying as the dam breaking was, the remarkable reporting efforts were not overlooked. Terry Drinkwater did such an outstanding job reporting live from the Telemobile that he was hired by *CBS News* shortly afterwards. Joe Benti, who anchored much of our extended coverage of the disaster, received wide acclaim for his work, and he too later left KTLA for an anchor position with *CBS News*. Tom Snyder was another reporter who received praise for his coverage, and he eventually moved on to *NBC News*, then to his very successful career as a network television and radio talk show host.

And in case you were wondering, it was a couple of weeks before Beverly and I got back to the store to pick up our Christmas gifts.

The Sinatra Kidnapping

I became news director just as some of the biggest news stories of the decade happened in America. In less than a month, I reported President John Kennedy's shooting in Dallas and the collapse of the Baldwin Hills Dam in L.A. I knew being a news director was going to be busy, but I never expected so much to happen so fast.

The third major story I covered in those formative months was the kidnapping of Frank Sinatra Jr. from his Los Angeles home in December, 1963. I, along with two dozen other cameramen and reporters, had been on the story from early that morning, after hearing news of a ransom demand. We'd spent the entire day racing around. We reported from the various phone booths in the city where the kidnappers had called from, before tearing off to various spots where the ransom money had been picked up. As the day wore on, we scoped out the different police stations in hopes of picking up some official news about Sinatra's release.

It was past midnight and freezing cold when we converged outside Frank Sinatra's Bel Air home. I stamped my feet a couple of times, pulled my coat closer to my neck, and jammed my cold hands deep into my overcoat pockets to endure the brisk winter evening. As is to be expected for a case such as this, there were countless rumors flying around about. Had a ransom been paid? Had Sinatra Jr. been released? Were the suspects still at large or had they been taken into custody? Was Frank Sinatra about to come outside with his son? What we did know was that there were too many secret things going on, and each reporter's news instinct brought him to the Sinatra home to unravel the main elements of the story.

We were about two hours into our frosty vigil in front of the Sinatra home when a couple of vans pulled into the driveway. Several men in tuxedos got out and began pulling out tables, benches and chairs. We were very curious when they brought out tablecloths and candelabras. The tables, complete with linen napkins and silverware, were set up on the damp grass next to the street. Trays of meat, cheese, fruit, salad, and bread appeared, along with stacked china and hot coffee.

The outdoor buffet was for the shivering newsmen. The men in tuxedos were waiters from Chasen's in Beverly Hills. Dave Chasen, the owner of the famous restaurant, was on the scene himself to make sure the buffet was just right and to see that the reporters had all the food and drink they wanted. Dave told us that Frank Sinatra had seen the large number of us outside and knew that we had to be cold and hungry. Sinatra called Chasen to get the formal buffet set up on his lawn and to try to make us all a little more comfortable. It was an elegant and classy thing to do, and I'll never forget it.

As it turned out, we never did get our story on that cold night. The Bel Air Patrol helped Frank Sinatra Jr. get away without talking to newsmen. The police hid him in the trunk of one of their patrol cars after his release by the kidnappers, then took him to their office about a mile away, where he hopped into a friend's car and left the scene.

I talked about that night with a fellow reporter friend who'd frozen along with the rest of us, and he wondered if the catered dinner was a diversion to get Sinatra Jr. away from the cameras and reporters. No one will ever know. As for me, I prefer to think of it as a delightful gesture from Frank Sinatra, who'd had more than his share of run-ins with the press. And besides, the roast beef was delicious.

CHAPTER 13

The Sixties Riots: The Nation is Shaken

Decades, like people, are difficult to classify in orderly categories. The troublesome undercurrents that had bubbled during the fifties exploded to the surface with the arrival of the new decade. The sixties were all about "out with the old and in with the new," and it was a challenge to be the news director during this time of chaos and sweeping change.

Looking back, it's easy to tick off the events that occurred in the late fifties that thrust the sixties into disorder and turmoil, and I was there to report them all:

- Russia continued their old, hard line policy against America after Stalin's death in 1953.
- The French lost a long and bitter war against the Viet Cong when Dien Bien Phu fell in 1954. An armistice was signed and the French pulled out their troops, leaving a festering vacuum in the area.
- The United States and mainland China came "eyeball to eyeball" over the tiny offshore islands of Quemoy and Matsu. It almost caused a war, but the crisis subsided.
- The H-bomb became a reality in 1954.
- United States peacekeeping forces were deployed during The Israeli–Egyptian War in 1956.
- Nikita Khrushchev became premier of the Soviet Union in 1957.
- Sputnik stunned Americans in October of that same year by beating us into space.
- Our Marines went ashore in Lebanon in 1958.
- Fidel Castro's communist regime came to power in Cuba in 1959.

- Vice President Richard Nixon and Premier Nikita Khrushchev had their famous kitchen debate in Moscow that same year.
- Francis Gary Powers' U-2 plane was shot down over Soviet air space. He was tried, convicted, and sentenced by a Soviet court, and sent to jail.
- The Cuban missile crisis moved us to the brink of atomic war. (I remember standing in front of a bank of Teletype machines in the newsroom at the climactic moments of the missile crisis. Bill Stout was next to me. We didn't talk, but simply stared at every word on the wire machines until we got word that the Soviets had turned around and pulled back.)
- The Vietnam War happened during the Eisenhower and Kennedy administrations when the US moved in to fill the vacuum the French had left in Vietnam.

The unbridled optimism of the fifties soured into doubt, exhaustion, and anger. The dream seemed to shatter, and no one was prepared for the results of that anger. Many were tired of the old ways. They didn't like the business world and the impersonal demands of industry. A job was merely something to be tolerated. Concerns about juvenile delinquency and drug use rose to the surface. Even the language changed.

KTLA was always selective and careful about stories we covered and the words we used on the air. If a news story on the UPI Teletype contained any material the audience might find offensive, it was clearly marked at the start with a slug that read, "EDITORS, NOTE CONTENTS" to protect radio news announcers.

Some television programs began airing daring interviews with prostitutes, pornographers, or drug users. The guests were hidden by shadows or masks, and were called by their first names only. These broadcasts weren't considered real news programs, but were thought to be shocking and sensational.

At the time, I was a combination news director and assignment editor, and each day I had to deal with these new forces making news for the first time. Hippies became newsworthy for the unrest they constantly caused. Our camera crews were busy recording the day-to-day encounters over issues like curfews, anti-war demonstrations, and campus unrest. Hippies were unpredictable and they got our attention. We got to know the leaders, who were happy to keep us informed of their upcoming demonstrations on countless college campuses and government buildings in the city.

Through them, our terminology changed. Negroes were now called blacks. Mexican-Americans were called Chicanos. The women's movement was growing and demanding attention. There were sit-ins at the Board of Education to protest injustices. Unfair housing practices were under attack from the new demonstrators. Long lines of protestors marched back and forth to show their anger.

Underground groups like the Weathermen threatened violence. Extreme racial groups fought the police. In fact, our camera crews were trapped in the midst of a full-scale gun battle that erupted outside a black extremist headquarters on Central Avenue in Los Angeles.

Others used intimidation to show their latent power and their disdain for the news media. Reporters and cameramen had to be searched by members of extremist groups before they were permitted to go inside and cover the news story. As an assignment editor, I didn't have time to look at the worthiness of each cause—I just concentrated on their *news*worthiness. Our Telecopter covered the stories from above while our camera crews were invariably right in the middle of much of the action.

The anti-war demonstrations grew more desperate as the number of students about to be drafted increased. We were covering President Lyndon Johnson's appearance at the Century Plaza Hotel in Los Angeles, and thousands of organized anti-war demonstrators showed up to protest the policies in Vietnam. A full-scale riot broke out while the President was inside the hotel.

Because of the extreme violence, the sixties weren't a pleasant time for me, and though I was in the middle of it, I don't recall that brutal era with any fondness. I'll admit many positive changes happened during that time, but the physical and emotional toll rocked the nation for decades.

Beset By Violence

We had become a society plagued with violence. Our reporter Dick Hathcock methodically covered the gruesome Charles Manson story as the gang members were captured one by one for the brutal murders of Sharon Tate and her friends. We had camera crews covering the arrests, the trial, and the "side bar" stories as the Manson gang was gradually broken up and put behind bars. We did frequent interviews on a street corner next to the Hall of Justice in Los Angeles where the women of the Manson clan who were not in jail set up housekeeping to protest the imprisonment of their leader.

On a personal level, I found these stories incredibly bizarre. As KTLA's news director, I found them newsworthy. We covered the dozens of horrific murders that were eventually attributed to serial killers, the Skid Row Slasher and the Hillside Strangler. As careful as these two had been, it was ironic that the Skid Row Slasher, who murdered his victims in flophouses and back alleys, was finally caught only because he dropped his wallet with his name in it at a crime scene. He'd tried to get away too fast.

As with the Skid Row Slasher, it took a mistake to catch the Hillside Strangler. It turned out that his auto body shop was in that general vicinity of the murders. I remember going to an overgrown gully, high on a lonely hillside overlooking a wide section of the city, where two of the Hillside Strangler's victims were found. I looked out in the distance at the places where five other victims had been found, and wondered what had become of us as a "civilized" society.

The idea of a civilized society also rummaged through my head when demonstrators were having a bad day. It was a violent time, and no one was spared. Camraman Ken Graue ran for his life down a Westwood street because demonstrators had turned ugly and were racing after him. He had his undeveloped news film in his hand and was trying to keep it away from the members of the mob. Some didn't like what he'd shot and were determined to get the film away from him. People stopped on the sidewalk and looked on in amazement as a grown man in a suit and tie raced past, followed by an angry group of college students clad in jeans and T-shirts. Thanks to the congestion on the streets, Ken was able to duck into the lobby of a theatre and hide behind the popcorn machine. He saved the film and probably his neck.

When we screened the film back at the station, we couldn't see anything different from what we'd shot dozens of times before. The crowd was apparently in an ugly mood that day and decided to vent its frustration on the nearest television reporter, which was not an unusual phenomenon in those days.

It was a strange time to be an assignment editor. I remember many mornings spent checking to see where the riot for the day might be, before scheduling stories for my film crews.

Campus Life Turned Upside Down
Southern California had its hot spots, like every city. The University of California at Los Angeles had a belligerent, active anti-war group. Their free-speech area was always filled with firebrand speakers calling for an end to something, and we were there to cover it. But it came with a caveat: in those days of riot coverage, it was sometimes difficult to know if we were covering the news as it was happening or actually *causing* the news because our cameras were there. For this reason, I insisted that our camera crews always keep a low profile.

Governor Reagan was holding a Regent's meeting at UCLA when a group unleashed a massive demonstration against him and the college administrators. Cameraman Ed Clark, who was in the middle of the demonstration, recommended we send the Telecopter because, as he said, "This thing might explode into a major riot."

I had the copter up in the air and on its way to UCLA in a matter of minutes. The campus at UCLA is filled with beautiful, flowing lawns and gardens, and is so large that the copter crew couldn't find the building where the demonstrators were haranguing the Governor and the Regents. They flew over the peaceful scene for ten minutes before they finally spotted the cluster of students bent on disrupting the meeting. How ironic. The big story of the day was on the turbulent UCLA campus, but from the air, everything appeared calm and pastoral.

A Different Approach

Tempers reached the boiling point during the Cambodian incursion by US troops in the Vietnam War. Angry students from many schools took to the streets, wreaking havoc wherever they went. The University of Southern California had been relatively quiet during these times, but this latest development stirred students there into action. USC had a large group who felt strongly about the "immoral action" of the government, and they wanted to get their position across. However, their approach was radically different than most of the students in the rest of the country: They invited the newsmen to lunch.

The lunch was held on campus and several newsmen were seated at each table. Each of the tables had a student spokesman talk one-on-one to the newsmen about the righteousness of his causes. It was an interesting give and take between the newsmen and the concerned students, and I came away from the briefing sessions feeling that the station should give these students some kind of a forum to express their case. Until that point there had been no worthwhile debate because face-to-face encounters always seemed to turn into shouting matches. Like the USC students had done, I wanted to try a different approach.

We took our cameras to USC and taped an emotional (and very one-sided) discussion among the students, which we ran on the air for twenty minutes. We also invited some national administration spokesmen to the studio so they could listen to what the students had to say. Then they came on the air to give the administration's rebuttal to the students' arguments.

In the following segment, the same students, now in another studio, responded live to the administration's position. By keeping the two sides in different studios, we were able to have a debate without the irrational fury that marked similar discussions. Administration officials summarized the evening and tried to point out areas of agreement.

We'd created a successful series. It ran for two hours each night for a week, and became a valuable public forum for the students to give their side of the discussion. Until then, they hadn't believed that anyone cared enough to listen to them. And, in turn, they had a chance to hear a rational, personal reply from the administration. It was an interesting back-and-forth that covered the policies being followed in Vietnam and what should be done in the future.

The administration sent out top people from Washington for the five-night series, but we needed a compliment of local experts to augment the administration's spokesmen. Everything went well until the fourth night, when the spokesmen for the administration's position were the chancellors from several local universities. No one questioned this choice because much of the turbulence had taken place on their campuses.

The students were well-mannered and made their points with conviction. They were against the war and they wanted the United States to pull out. Much to my shock, the chancellors agreed with almost every point the students made. My carefully balanced show had tilted all the way to the students' side. So much for a fair representation of opposing views. The next night I made sure my foreign policy experts were more in line with the government's position.

All the unrest did manage to have a lighter side. I recall one demonstration of UCLA students who decided to stage a sit-in on Wilshire Boulevard to bring their cause to the attention of the media. There were hundreds of them sitting in the middle of the street, completely closing down the flow of traffic. Police moved in with their riot gear and began arresting them quietly, one by one. They were assisted to their feet, walked to a nearby bus, and booked. UCLA basketball star Bill Walton was still sitting on the boulevard, and I leaned over to one of the lieutenants and said, "Be very careful when you pick up Walton. He has a big game tomorrow night."

In 1954, Chambers was emcee of Frosty Frolics, a weekly musical ice show televised from the Winter Garden in Pasadena

Stan Chambers and co-writer, Lynn Price pose with Stan's star on Hollywood Blvd.

Stan Chambers winner of the Golden Mike Award

Klaus Landsberg, the man with great vision who started it all at KTLA.

In 1952, KTLA cameras were ten miles from ground zero when the A-bomb tests were televised from the Nevada desert.

Stan Chambers covering a refinery fire

This is a scene from *The Return of the Amazing Colossal Man* in 1958, Stan's one and only motion picture role.

Stan Chambers covering the arrival of the *Spruce Goose* at the Port of Long Beach.

Stan at the Rose Parade with Art Linkletter and Bill Cosby

Stan with his camera crew

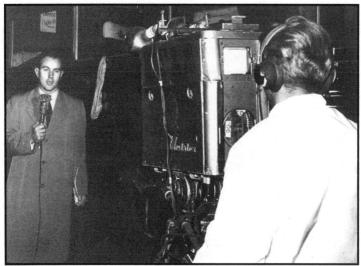

Stan reporting

Stan and Roy Disney

Stan interviewing military personnel

Stan taking notes for a breaking story

Stan Chambers with Tom Brokaw at KTLA's signature broadcast of
the Tournament of Roses Parade.

Stan Chambers with Regis Philbin at KTLA's signature broadcast of
the Tournament of Roses Parade.

Stan Chambers and Los Angeles mayor, Tony Villaraigosa, at the luncheon honoring Stan for 58 years of broadcasting in 2005.

In 1997, Los Angeles Mayor Richard Riordan presented Stan with a Los Angeles City street sign that was posted just outside the KTLA studios, at the corner of Sunset and Van Ness.

Stan and his grandson, Jaime, who is also reporter with KTLA, in front of
the Stan Chambers Building at KTLA which was dedicated in 1997

The 1990KTLA News At Ten team. Anchors Hal Fishman and Jann Carl
in front. Stan Chambers, Larry McCormick, and Stu Nahan in back.

Vice President-elect Richard Nixon and his wife, Pat, being interviewed at the 1953 Rose Parade. Nixon was Grand Marshall in 1959 and 1960

Stan and his wife, Gege, at the luncheon celebrating his 58 years with KTLA.

Stan Chambers and his eleven children.

Stan is surrounded by his grandchildren for their traditional Christmas story reading.

CHAPTER 14
KTLA Adds More Influence

In December of 1965, there were some big changes at *KTLA News*. George Putnam, who had been broadcasting at KTTV since 1952, moved to the station. As was predicted, he became an immediate hit.

Although quite conservative, George was the most popular reporter on television with the minorities of Southern California. He tried to tell their stories and address out their problems. He always accentuated the positive. He became a champion of their causes and put his personal effort into many fights to right some wrongs. He tried to stop what he considered serious ills from spreading further into society.

I remember walking into the studio one day and seeing about fifty people on the news stage dressed in the garb of the captive nations of Lithuania, Latvia, and Estonia. It was George's idea to invite them to appear on his newscast that night because it was Captive Nations Week. This had been observed since the Eisenhower years, but now the government was no longer giving it any special recognition. George felt that by ignoring Captive Nations Week after so many years of observing it, we were turning our backs on millions of people held behind the Iron Curtain. This was his protest to the President and the Congress.

It was a moving presentation. Men and women sang proudly, bringing back painful memories of those left behind. They reinforced the message that there were so many people that were unable to leave their countries, who lived as captives under the brutal heel of the Soviets. George thought this was a very important message, and he couldn't figure out why the President and Congress didn't think so, too.

George was always emotionally affected by the issues of the day. He tried to help the underdog, the person who never got a fair deal from society. He was one of the first television journalists to reach out to different communities and to try to help them with their problems. There are former gang members, grandfathers today, who were helped by George Putnam. He worked with them to break their gang cycle ten years before the civil rights efforts of the mid-sixties. He helped black reporters get jobs in television years before the broadcast industry caught up with him and started to hire minorities.

He stood for the old values of right and wrong, good and bad, and because of this, he had a loyal following in the ethnic communities. He became concerned when young activists from those communities took radical stands against what their parents believed, and was hurt when those radicals considered him unfaithful to their cause. He debated them and questioned their ways throughout the turbulent sixties.

George crusaded against drug use when it was still little-known to the majority of the population, and he warned about the spread of drugs among young people. He wrote editorials, commentaries, and news stories pointing out the dreadful consequence of a drug-infested society.

George got very involved in his news coverage and never sat back while things crumbled around him. He was a crusader of the old school of reporters, and people loved him for it. He couldn't walk down Hollywood Blvd. without hearing shouts of, "Give it to them, George!" "We're behind you all the way!" "Keep up the good work!"

Predictably, he had a large and dedicated following among law enforcement because he understood the problems they faced. They were among his most loyal supporters. Anytime I was out on a story, I would always hear from officers, "How's George?" "Say hello to George for me. He's doing a great job." "Putnam knows what's happening, and I'm glad there's someone to tell others what's really going on." "Putnam's the best."

George was always at the center of controversy, and his large audience was comprised of those who couldn't stand him as well as those who thought he was the brightest reporter on the air. He aired his personal feelings and comments on "One Reporter's Opinion," which he called his mid-spot because it always came halfway through the broadcast. He dissected the controversial issues of the day and wasn't at all afraid to air his feelings. Because his opinions drew such widespread interest, he converted the last section of his news broadcast to an open forum for the studio audience and called it *Talk Back*.

Hal Fishman and Larry McCormick, who did the newscast with George, were also on *Talk Back*. The three of them faced the audience and tackled the volatile subjects of the day. It was a refreshing departure from the usual newscast because it gave people a chance to react to the news that had happened that day. *Talk Back* was always filled with tension as people spoke about prevalent issues that affected our lives. There were some great arguments between George and the audience, and he went toe-to-toe with those who disagreed with him, and battled it out.

One of George's finest hours was during the coverage of the Deadwyler inquest in the mid-sixties. It started as a high-speed chase in South Central Los Angeles when Leonard Deadwyler was seen rushing his pregnant wife to the hospital. As was common in the South, he attached a white piece of clothing to his antenna to show that he was going on an emergency run. The local police weren't familiar with the practice and gave chase. He was stopped and killed when a Los Angeles police officer stuck his cocked weapon into the car and it discharged. Because racial tensions were already high, the tragic event threatened to touch off a riot.

On the first day of the inquest, people surged in the corridors outside the courtroom, becoming loud and disruptive when they were unable to get into the hearing room. Lloyd Sigmon, a Golden West Broadcasting executive, asked me to find out if there was any way KTLA could televise the inquest to reduce tensions in the city. I called District Attorney Evelle Younger and told him of Lloyd's concern.

"Stan, I have been thinking the same thing. I was wondering if there was any chance that some station would televise the inquest."

I felt as if all the cards had fallen right into place. "We're ready to go right away," I told him.

Evelle Younger phoned me back in minutes, giving KTLA permission. This was highly unusual because cameras weren't allowed inside courtrooms in those days. The inquest was transferred to the largest courtroom available to make room for KTLA's two television cameras.

By this time, the public was aware of George Putnam's soothing effect on the city and that he was defined by fairness and honesty. People watched the developments, comforted that nothing could be covered up. I had the pleasure of sharing reporting duties with George that day and watching the public's emotional tensions subside. The fate was sealed when a physiologist was brought in to verify that a man thrown off balance would tend to make a reflexive clutching movement that could pull a trigger. The police officer was exonerated and the shooting was listed as a tragic accident

Talking Heads or Visuals?

In 1967, KTTV gave George Putnam an offer he couldn't refuse, and he switched stations. In turn, KTLA selected the well-known and popular Los Angeles police chief, Tom Reddin, as the new anchorman.

Putnam was strong and flamboyant, and there was more emphasis on his personality than the news film during his years with KTLA. His departure made me think about how things needed to be changed.

We still had a relatively small staff during those years. Although I was news director at the time, I spent my mornings as assignment editor in order to get a jump on the news day. I was able to see what was happening, get a good hold on developments, and send camera crews to the important stories.

Looking back on those years, I now see that I spent too much time covering what I considered the important news, and didn't worry about whether it was visual or not. If the story seemed important, I sent a camera crew. This was the purist's position in television journalism, but it created problems for the overall newscast. Put five important stories together and you would, more than likely, end up with five "talking heads" following each other on the broadcast.

The plague of the talking head originated in the traditional news conference. Most news people believed that if there was a news conference, it was because some spokesman had something new and important to say, and the media should be there to cover it. The news conference syndrome became such a habit that I often found myself sending a crew to the Los Angeles Press Club to cover a news conference at 9:00, another one at 10:00, and a third one at 11:00. Most of the other television stations would be there as well.

It was difficult to rationalize chasing after stories that were more visual and less substantial. We did a few features and light stories to break up the chain of talking heads, but I often questioned whether the light, pleasant story was really news or was a cream puff—a meaningless feature—or worse, a public relations stunt. Sportscaster Dick Enberg summed it up best when he complained about the timing of his sports section in the newscast. He said, "My spot always follow the animal story from the zoo."

Our station manager, John Reynolds, gave me a terrific analogy describing how to handle this problem. He said that a newscast is like a special meal: there are meat and potatoes for the main course, but there should also be the appetizers, dessert, and all the other minutiae that make up a memorable meal. It should also be prepared well, with the right trimmings and atmosphere. I took that advice to heart. When I looked at some visual story that didn't have the importance of meat and potatoes, but could be served for dessert after dinner, I covered it. Pictures are the vital element in a television newscast. It is important to take advantage of the visual possibilities of the television screen.

Going To the Dogs

One of the stories I did was almost too visual.

For many years, the Los Angeles Police Department did not use dogs to flush out suspects. There was a time when the image of a policeman using a dog was too reminiscent of the early civil rights marches in the South, when dogs were misused in controlling crowds. However, a group of LAPD officers wanted to prove how helpful dogs could be for finding hidden suspects. A dog could search a warehouse in minutes, where officers might take hours to complete the same task.

The police department decided on a pilot program. Each dog was thoroughly trained by its master, who was an officer. The dog lived with the policeman, was part of the officer's family, played with his children, and went go to work with the officer at night. This was the start of the K-9 Corps, and we did a story on it. We watched the officers put their dogs through a series of training exercises. They searched deserted buildings, responded to various commands, and were always under control. It was a purely visual story.

I wanted to show how gentle the dogs were at home with the officers, how they were lovable pets for children and became members of the family. I worked out a scene for our story where the dog would put his paws on my shoulders and I would pet him as I closed off the segment. Police dogs are big; when they stand on their hind legs, their front paws easily rest on an adult's shoulders, bringing their head at eye level with yours.

Cameraman Joe Dylan gave me my cue and he started rolling his camera. I gave the command; the dog stood on his hind legs and placed his paws on my shoulders, his tongue hanging out in a sloppy grin. At that moment I made the wrong move, and somehow stepped on his hind paw. The dog let out a loud howl, looked straight at me, and lunged. His teeth nearly brushed my face. Before I could wonder whether he'd tear my throat out, his forepaws abruptly slid down from my shoulder, and he walked away.

The film shows my startled, horrified face as the dog growled, gnashed his teeth and instinctively defended himself. Phil Leask, the editor who put the story together, rolled the color film frame by frame for me. The dog's training saved me. Like any animal, he responded to pain in an instinctive manner, but caught himself because of his discipline.

I have watched in awe over the years as those dogs catch suspect after suspect in dark, strange places. Having been up close and personal with their teeth, I certainly understand why so many suspects give up when they see the K-9 Corps on the scene.

Color and Budgets

The advent of color film gave us all a new appreciation of the importance of the picture when telling a story. However, one of the continuous problems I had as news director was isolation. I was so involved in the newscasts and problems, I was often unable look ahead at what was going to happen in the industry. It was just as difficult to look around at other stations and keep close tabs on what they were doing. While I had my head buried in the production of each broadcast, there was much going on that I wasn't aware of.

One of those was color film, which was becoming commonplace. Unfortunately, I was too well-trained in the local station mentality, which says that that if it's new, it costs money, and we don't have a budget for it. Expenses always had to be kept down, so we usually had to make do with what we had.

Because of this, we rarely used color film, and, if we did, it was usually footage from Vietnam. But new techniques to make the news program more visual were being introduced. Full-time artists were being added to staffs to make the programs more attractive to viewers. More reporters were being added, and the scope of news was being expanded. Despite all the changes, I remained in a mostly meat and potatoes world.

My tunnel vision in those years kept me at my desk. I had my Telecopter crew on duty, and we did live coverage of stories almost every day, while other stations were just starting to experiment with it. We were doing reasonably well and, especially given the extreme limitations of my budget, I felt I didn't have much to learn from the others. I was trapped in the past, not realizing that changes were about to explode all around me.

I'd heard of electronic breakthroughs, but assumed that they were the concern of the engineering department. I was one of the first news directors in the country to use a mini-cam crew every day. It was the one we used in our helicopter. I failed to see the time when all cameras would be mini-cams. If someone had suggested it then, my first reaction would have been: They cost too much and we can't afford them.

I had trouble getting money to keep my film cameras repaired and operating. I had only one film editor and his assistant to edit all of our film. I had a live Telemobile and a live Telecopter; why should I need more? We had one transmitter for our live units at the time, and I figured that was enough for any station. I didn't foresee that almost everyone would have three or four in the near future.

It was 1970, and I had heard rumors from the front office that changes might be made. I knew no one could do the job better than I, but still, I had an uneasy feeling, and it gnawed at me.

Sitting behind the assignment desk in the newsroom always made me envious of the reporters who went out to do the stories. They did what I wanted to do. I put up with newsroom assignments because the work had to be done, and I figured I could do it better than anyone else. However, when I had a chance to go back into the field, I was delighted. A desk job was work; reporting was fun. Field reporting is the best part of television news, the real world, where I wanted to be.

But that isn't to say that leaving the news directorship was easy. Sure, with the advantage of 20/20 hindsight, I can see the reasons for the changes that took place over the years. When I left the news director spot, the biggest improvement my successor, Bill Fyffe, made the push to triple the news department budget. Television was, and still is, an expensive business, and it was necessary to spend money to make money. His was a sound and daring move after my years at the helm, when the philosophy was: The less you spent, the better you were doing the job. Bill asked me to stay on his staff as a general reporter. Although I was sorry to be stepping down, I accepted his offer.

It turned out to be the best thing I ever did.

CHAPTER 15
A New Career and a Chance to Travel

It was good to get away from KTLA for a few days and enjoy the Super Bowl. I was concerned about the changes taking place at the station, and this weekend was a good chance to put things into perspective. After working for so long, I suddenly felt my career drifting, and ominously quiet. Sometimes it's the ordinary things that rescue you, pull you back to reality, and point you in the right direction.

The ordinariness of home life gave me a chance to take a step back and reflect on things. No job can be fulfilling all the time, and news is a bruising business. I'd been knocked down, but I let the pain wear off and I got back up. That morning with my family reminded me of what was real and to enjoy it because there was still so much ahead. I knew the emotional hurt would heal.

The news business is ever-changing. If I looked on the bright side, fine-tuned my attitude, and kept plugging ahead, I knew I'd carve a new career. What more could I ask for than to return to reporting?

Back In the Saddle

One of my favorite jobs was being the action reporter, a consumer advocate for our viewers. It stirred up a lot of viewer interest and gave me a chance to get a new perspective on people I met while covering news stories. I was in more living rooms than an aggressive insurance salesman. This was all part of the station's intention to show viewers that we cared about them and would help them whenever we could. Their letters came flooding into the station, asking if we could help solve any number of problems. Carmel Denton, who was the entire action reporter staff, would get to work on it, and in a few weeks she usually resolved the problem. In those cases, we'd bring our cameras into the viewer's living rooms and interview them about their particular problem and how it was fixed. Several times a week, I would visit houses of people who had been helped.

Carmel solved a wide variety of viewers' headaches, from lost veterans and social security checks to washing machines or refrigerators that companies had failed to repair. The list was lengthy and varied, but she always seemed to find a solution. In truth, it wasn't magic. The station would get a letter outlining the problem, and Carmel would copy it and send it to the president of the company in question along with a form letter from the KTLA action reporter. That was it. As benign as it was, company presidents understood the value of good publicity, and fixed the particular problem. They wanted to show that these complaints were taken quite seriously.

As little as I had to do with the actual nuts and bolts of making things right, I never got tired of hearing, "Nothing happened until I wrote to KTLA and the action reporter got to work on this. In two weeks, a nice letter came from the company telling me that everything was settled. I want to thank you and KTLA for all you did."

This repeated itself night after night, with different varieties of gratitude expressed each time. People were beginning to believe I could do anything. In reality, of course, it was all Carmel.

Since I was doing my regular news reporting every day as well, Carmel worked out a great system for the action reporter interviews. She checked what area I was assigned to for that day, then went through her file of completed action reporter cases to give me addresses of people we'd helped. If the film crew and I finished our news assignment early enough, we would go over to a house in the neighborhood and film an action reporter story.

Travel

The mid-seventies were great travel years for me, when I was sent to Japan, Guatemala, Canada, and England. Overseas trips are great but always a challenge. It's not easy going through customs with twenty pieces of luggage and not losing any of them. Nor is it a picnic trying to ship your videotapes to Los Angeles and finding out that it can't be done on the weekends from the country you're in. But aside from the irritations and hardships of doing foreign interviews, there's the flip side of visiting the ruins of Tikal in the Guatemala jungles, standing over the tomb of Oliver Cromwell inside Westminster Abbey in London, or getting close-up film of Her Royal Majesty, Queen Elizabeth II.

Here's the setting for that last one: Dark wooden beams crisscrossed the ceiling and the white straw-and-plaster walls of the pub. Ornate pieces of brass hung as sentries from the rough oak mantle. Overstuffed chairs and couches formed a homey half-circle in front of the newly lit fireplace. Waltzing flames caressed the crackling logs in the soot-dusted hearth of brick and stone, warming everyone who entered. Why on earth would anyone leave this place to go out into the cold overcast English countryside on this dreary October afternoon in 1975?

Her Majesty was making a ceremonial visit to the small island of Runnymede as part of the celebration of the signing of the Magna Carta by King John and his noblemen 760 years before. She'd boarded her yacht earlier that morning and sailed down the Thames. This was an ideal opportunity for us to film a news story on the beautiful English countryside, see the excited townspeople, and get close-up film of Her Majesty as she greeted her subjects. The small, open cabin boat was only large enough for a cameraman, a sound man, and the pilot, who would guide them along the way. We had little choice but to leave our camera crew, Gil Donaldson and Sy Klein, in the boat that was following the Queen.

My producer Lew Rothbart, and I were disappointed we couldn't all fit aboard and view royalty close-up, so we did the next best thing: we drove our car along the route to the various towns.

We stood in the crowd and watched the enthusiastic reception the townspeople gave to the Queen. Then, as the royal party departed, we jumped back in our car and drove to the next village. We always arrived considerably ahead of the royal flotilla, so we would stop and go into the town pub and wait for the small task force to arrive.

Lew and I enjoyed the frothy taste of English ale. Our host and driver, Bruce Higgens, had a great time showing us the various taverns along the Thames while regaling us with the historical importance of each pub.

While it was warm and comfortable for the three of us in the pubs that dotted our route, it was cold, damp, and drizzling for Gil and Sy in their open boat. The moisture kept fogging the camera lens, so Gil was constantly drying it with lens paper. When the film was later developed, the dampness on the lens created a soft, warm, gauze-like tone, and gave the Queen, the flotilla, and the countryside an unreal quality, as if they were part of a medieval picture.

The film magic did nothing to raise the spirits of the freezing camera crew, however. The biting cold and the pervasive dampness grew more severe with each town. They huddled together in the bobbing boat with no protection from the elements except their thin California jackets.

On the other hand, Lew and I grew mellower as we hit country pub after country pub. We had no problem enjoying the beer and appreciating the pageantry of Her Majesty's arrival. We were invited to a beautiful cottage that rested on the tip of a small island in the Thames. It was a perfect spot to get a close-up look at the Queen. Her boat would pass right in front of the house, and she'd be so close, we would almost be able to reach out and touch the royal craft.

As the parade of boats came nearer, we prepared to go outside and get as close as possible to the Queen. However, the excitement of the moment proved to be too much for two young mothers in the crowd. "Would you mind?" a tall brunette asked as she handed me her baby. Shocked, I took him.

"How nice of you two," the other mother said, as she handed her child to Lew.

"Are you sure you don't mind?" the brunette asked, not waiting for an answer as they raced out the door.

Lew and I exchanged perplexed expressions as we jiggled our charges on our shoulders while staring out the cabin window. Whoever said reporters are arrogant never played babysitter to two English children while the Queen floated by. It could have been worse: After the Queen's flotilla passed by, we caught a glimpse of our camera crew bundled up in their open boat, Gil wiping the lens of his camera.

Even though Gil and Sy nursed colds for the rest of the trip, the news stories they filmed were wonderfully visual and creative. Thanks, guys, you really took one for the team.

CHAPTER 16

The Seventies: Murders, Muggings, and Coping

The country staggered into the seventies, battered from the blows of the sixties. Changes had been unleashed that would affect the nation for years to come.

- The heated anti-war fever was contagious and continued to take its toll on the nation's morale. Disenchanted veterans came home to mixed welcomes.
- A gas shortage startled the nation and left desperate drivers waiting in long lines for hours.
- Inflation exploded throughout the country along with a growing recession.
- President Nixon stunned the world twice with his surprise trip to China and his resignation in the wake of the Watergate investigations.
- Sky Lab and the Voyagers were rocketed on their space missions.
- There were the Sandinistas in Nicaragua, the Ayatollah Khomeini in Iran, a Soviet expeditionary force in Afghanistan, and a dozen wars and revolutions creating strife throughout the world.
- John Travolta became a bright new star with *Saturday Night Fever*. Martina Navratilova, from communist Czechoslovakia, dominated the tennis world, and USC's O.J. Simpson became a football star.

Gangs Hit the Streets

One of the most telling developments in this country in the seventies was the rise of violent urban crime. It was all too frequent a scene for our cameras: Another gang killing shattered the late afternoon in the deteriorating section of East Los Angeles. The bodies of two people lay under white sheets sprawled on the street. They had been standing by the curb, drinking beer and working on their cars, when rival gang members sped by and opened fire.

Homicide investigators and members of the Los Angeles Police Department's gang bureau were already there when our television news crews appeared on the scene. Residents looked upon the invasion of the police and press like a circus setting up tents, and we knew it would be difficult to talk to witnesses through the usual waving into the television cameras and shoving to get behind us as we did our live shots. Sadly, there was little concern for the two boys lying in the street next to their broken-down car, with the hood still up and the driver's door open.

While the homicide detectives investigated the murder, officers swept the area for witnesses. We were restricted in what we could cover because witnesses had to be taken to the police station. Nonetheless, we talked to people to see what we could find out. To my surprise, my crew and I found a girl named Amelia who lived two houses away, knew the two boys, and had seen the drive-by shooting. She agreed to let me interview her on camera.

"Doug and Ricardo were fixing their car," she began. "There was the sound of a car racing up the street. I turned and looked. It slowed down as it passed the two guys. I think there were four or five shots. The guys in the car screamed something. Then they burned rubber and sped away. The two guys standing next to the broken-down car fell to the pavement. One of them, Doug, tried to reach up to the car door, but he just toppled onto the street."

"Could you see who was in the car?"

"Sure, they were all Brown Doggers. That's a bad gang. I know two of them from last year in school. I know who they are."

By this time, it was a madhouse with all the neighborhood kids jumping around, waving and making faces in front of the camera, so I thanked her and ended the interview. The kids followed my cameraman and sound man as they went back down the street to get other pictures. It dawned on me that no other camera crew had discovered that Amelia was a witness. If the camera crews hadn't found her, that meant the police hadn't either. I walked back to her, without a camera or microphones. "Amelia, can I talk to you for moment?"

She smiled. "Sure."

"You have to be more careful what you say about gangs. You just told me you know who the killers are, and that could be very dangerous. Tell the police, but no one else."

She tossed her hair. "Those Brown Doggers don't scare me."

"If they think you know who killed the two boys, they could cause you a lot of trouble. Never say you can identify the killers. I won't use it on the air, but others might, so take care."

She just looked at me.

"No hard feelings?" I asked.

She shook her head. "No, none."

"Thanks," I said. "Thanks for the interview. I just won't use that part."

"I'll be more careful," she said, smiling.

Later, as the coroner was taking the bodies off the street, I saw Amelia on the steps of her house watching the scene. Her family peered out the front door and through the windows.

I looked at all the neighbors, the graffiti, the youthful exuberance amid all the sadness. I wondered if Amelia might tell others she knew who the killers were. I was reasonably certain no reporter would run a clip like that, but if only one did, Amelia could be the next victim.

As I walked back to our camera car, I kept thinking about it. We have a very serious responsibility to the people we interview. We have to use good sense and good taste in determining what we put on the air. We want the best and most interesting material, but we can never jeopardize the safety of a person who might have told you too much.

Is that censoring the news? Is that holding back something that people have a right to know? I don't think so. I believe it's just good news judgment. The police have to know, but I don't think the whole world does.

I haven't encountered many situations like this, but when I do, I proceed with caution. My motto is, "If in doubt, don't run it." Journalists must check everything out to make sure it's accurate. Never shoot from the hip just to beat your competitors on other stations. Be sure first; otherwise we have the ability to hurt a lot of people.

Stolen Property, Broken Hearts

Doing theft stories was tough. It's frustrating to do a story on recovered stolen property and actually see all the people who were ripped off. Standing in the midst of the victims, you can feel the human toll these burglaries take. This was just one night of a public display of the stolen articles. Thousands visited the display room at the Van Nuys Police Station to try to locate their possessions. Many were successful, but many weren't.

Each victim had his own story of how terrified he was to come home and find his place ransacked and his stereos, television sets, jewelry, and silver gone. The terrifying questions were always there: Would the robbers come back again? What if they tried to break in when someone was at home? Would they have a gun? Would they use it? These victims were of all ages, all colors, all backgrounds, and were brought here by a common harrowing experience.

As bad as the street crimes are, the robbers and muggers are the most feared. They strike with random violence and prey on those least able to protect themselves. They use any available weapon, and care nothing about the victims. Only their money.

Gunshots

The sounds of gunshots always brought real fear to those of us who covered the streets because it was always unexpected. But even though it froze my blood, there was something about being in the middle of a breaking story that superseded my baser instincts to run.

I remember once being at the scene of a barricade at a Western Avenue motel. The suspect was holed up in the motel, and he had shot his rifle out of an open window earlier in the day, so officers moved all us newsmen across the street for safety. It was dark now, and they worried he might aim at the clustered newsmen and cameramen.

I had left the group to call the newsroom from a pay phone down the street. I could see all of the cameramen and reporters on a side street using the edge of the corner building as protection, when the blast of a gunshot sent all the stoic newsmen diving for the ground. It was pure reflex. (To this day I'll never be able to fathom the cameramen's natural instinct to keep their cameras high so they wouldn't be damaged when the cameraman dropped to the sidewalk. Just as natural as breathing, cameramen protect their cameras at all cost.) Realizing the gunman had missed his target, everyone slowly got up and retreated to a safer spot. Since I was down the street and out of the line of fire, I could appreciate the imminent danger everyone had faced. But it was also pretty funny watching a bunch of journalists hit the deck.

No one was hurt that night, and the suspect was killed the next morning when he tried to take hostages out of the motel and make a getaway.

The Lighter Side

Violence is unexpected and dangerous, but it can also have a lighter side. I remember one time I was in New York I came across two cab drivers who were going head to head, yelling and screaming at each other, just moments from blows. I walked up and asked if they could tell me where the Plaza Hotel was. They stopped their argument mid-sentence and gave me detailed directions. Surprisingly enough, they broke off their argument after that, and went their separate ways.

Once when I was covering a stakeout in South Central Los Angeles, my crew and I briefly became a part of the action. Camera cars were parked at a street corner, and the crews were waiting for something to happen. I was sitting in our camera truck with my cameraman, Martin Clancy, when I noticed a man trying to get my attention through the window. He had borrowed money from me earlier and had become a pest. Before I knew what was happening, he opened my door, reached over me, picked up the portable scanner on the seat, and ran off. Martin and I were too stunned to do anything. We sat there in the front seat and watched, open mouthed, as the man took off in a dead run across the street.

Dave Lopez, a cameraman from KMEX-TV who later came to KTLA, saw him running and tried to stop him. He ducked just as the man took a swipe at him with the scanner.

"Let's follow him in the van," I told Martin.

"I'll have the station call the police," he said, turning the key in the ignition. He pulled out onto Figueroa just as the man looked over his shoulder and disappeared down a side street.

We drove slowly, working our way through the traffic to get into the left turn lane.

"Ken Davis, this is EJ-2."

"Go ahead EJ-2," came the immediate reply.

"Call the police, tell them that a radio scanner was stolen from us and we are following the suspect down Figueroa just south of Vernon."

"Are you okay?"

"Yeah, we're all right. Now he's running east on the first block south of Vernon."

We turned down the street and saw him running down at the end of the block before disappearing behind the house on the corner. We picked up speed and turned the corner, and I saw him hiding behind a gold Cadillac. We passed him, pulled into a driveway, and turned around in time to see him retrace his steps. He passed the Channel 9 minivan that had joined us in the hunt. They saw him and turned around.

The Channel 2 minivan stopped in the middle of the street as the man ran by. The Channel 4 minivan was waiting for him at the corner. He saw the van ahead and ducked in between houses. A boy watching the chase ran over to the now-breathless man and grabbed the scanner out of his hands, then raced down the street toward us. The man, now jogging slowly, ran up a driveway and into a backyard.

It was over. We got the radio back and let the suspect get away. We saw him come out from behind a house and continue to run south on Figueroa. For all I know, he ran clear to Cleveland. I thanked everyone for the help while Clancy gave the little guy five dollars for his heroics. Unbelievably, the scanner came through unscathed.

We all assembled back at our original location and swapped stories about the chase, eventually laughing at how bizarre the situation must have looked. Chasing a man down the street with our white television vans loaded with dishes and antennas on their roofs, turning corners, backing up, making U-turns, and almost crashing into each other must have looked like a scene out of *Keystone Cops*.

The punch line came as I was in the process of calling the station to tell them what had happened, and I overheard the tail end of a police radio broadcast, ". . . that's a roger, the suspect was being chased by four television news crews."

Coping

One of the most difficult times for reporters is when we visit a home hit by tragedy. It is especially painful when the house you visit is the home of a boy who police suspect is a criminal. How do you talk to a mother or father about their son who has just been picked up and is accused of killing several people, or doing some other despicable thing?

It's a difficult situation for the reporter. To tell the story properly, we need an on-camera interview. In most cases, the parents refuse to talk, and we end up expending a lot of time and energy trying to get a story we knew ahead of time we probably wouldn't get.

A newspaper reporter can go to the house and try to get some comments from the parents standing behind a half-open door. Even if they are reluctant to talk, they will often say a few things the reporter can include in his account. However, to get the story on television, we have to get people's permission before we can put them on camera. It can get tricky because they often don't want their faces on the ten o'clock news. But sometimes it's actually not as bad as it seems.

I remember one report where I had to visit the home of a mass murder suspect. We drove slowly through a prosperous neighborhood and stopped in front of a big white colonial house with newly painted green shutters. I walked along the well-groomed grass, climbed the front steps, and knocked on the door. After a long wait, it slowly opened.

I introduced myself. The tall, distinguished-looking father nodded. He opened the door all the way. "I wanted to talk to you about your son," I said. "Is he still in custody?"

The father nodded again. "Yes."

This is where an interview can go one of several ways, with anger, violence, and frustration being the likeliest outcomes. The hardest is the resigned defeatism of a puzzled and unbelieving parent. I'd learned to be prepared for any or all of them.

He paused before speaking, "My son didn't do anything. He wasn't worried about anything. I can always tell when he has something to hide. We spent most of the day painting the hallway. When it was time to drive down to the park to pick up his brother, I asked him to do it. He put his paint brush down on the can and took the car keys off the table and left."

"Are you concerned?" I asked.

"Of course I'm concerned. My boy is in jail. From what I can gather, he drove into an area where police had a stakeout for someone who looked like my son. They arrested him. He didn't do anything. Come in. I'll show you where we were painting."

I followed him to the end of the hallway, just where it opened into the breakfast room. "That's his brush over there on top of the paint can," he said, pointing to the partially painted walls, the open paint cans, and the drop cloths still on the floor. "See, he just finished that section of the wall."

I asked if he was willing to tell me his story on camera. "I'll show what the two of you were doing and you can tell me why you believe he is innocent."

"I *know* he is innocent," the father replied firmly.

We ran the interview with the father on our broadcast that night, and showed the unfinished painting job. "My boy will be all right," the father said. "He's done nothing. He couldn't have."

His son was released the next day.

Two Sides of the Coin

I think there are times when you grow as a reporter due to experiences that would never make it onto the air. Those emotional moments are yours alone, and most are so personal that they can be difficult to talk about. Yet those moments, those memories, are the very substance of our experiences, and are often called into play. They exist, but they leave a vacuum inside. They make you want to do something to change things, but you know there is really nothing you can do.

I had those feelings the night I watched a traffic sweep for drunk drivers that had been set up on Santa Monica Boulevard in Hollywood. A little boy was clutching a videotape as he stood amid the general chaos of countless police officers on motorcycles and the red and blue flashing lights of the police cars. He had been to a video rental store with his family. Since he was the only one who could speak English, he had picked out the video and paid the cashier. He was still holding the tape in his hand when his older brother slowed to a stop and followed the cars in front of him to the sobriety checkpoint.

A police officer leaned towards the driver's window of the Chevrolet. "We are conducting a sobriety check to see if anyone might be driving under the influence."

The brother, who didn't understand English, nodded his head. The scent of liquor was strong. I watched the officer motion the driver to turn onto a side street where motorists who were suspected of being drunk were being tested.

"May I have a Spanish-speaking officer over here?" the policeman called out to the command post.

The brother failed the test while his family sat in the car. He weaved and couldn't walk in a straight line. There was no doubt that he was very drunk. He was walked across to a mobile unit outfitted with a breathalyzer and other equipment that could confirm the officer's suspicions. I soon lost sight of him in the crowd and followed my cameraman around as we recorded various shots of what was going on as the checkpoint operated.

Later, I saw the family standing on the sidewalk as their now-impounded car was being towed to the police garage. The little boy put his hands on his crying mother's shoulders. To this day, I still see the video in the boy's hand as he tried to help his mother.

Almost forty other drivers were arrested and booked for DUI that night. Their stories differed, but the end result was the same; society had declared war on the drunk driver.

Drunk drivers were the reason we had our cameras outside City Hall one cold December night. A podium with a loudspeaker had been set up on a level of the First Street steps in the park surrounding City Hall. Mothers Against Drunk Driving was holding its annual candlelight vigil, and most of those in the crowd had lost a loved one to a drunk driver. Their pain was visible on their faces as they held pictures of those cut down before their time. The stories were catastrophic and heartbreaking, and those holding candles in the darkness would carry the tragedy with them for the rest of their lives.

I'll always remember one mother holding a picture of a little boy who had been killed by a drunk driver six months prior. Bitter tears flowed down her cheeks as she talked about the accident.

What struck me was that her son looked so much like the little boy holding the videocassette at the sobriety checkpoint. It was devastating to behold.

You span extremes when you are out there where the world unfolds. You are sent to a scene because something newsworthy has happened, and many have been caught by random chance in a mesh that suddenly wraps tightly around them. Being there when things are happening helps you mature as a reporter. You never know what your next assignment will be, but you wait until you get your next call and your assignment editor sends you racing across town to another human situation.

News is the unusual, the exceptional, the uncommon occurrence that takes place in our daily lives. That is why so much of it is bad. As a reporter, you are often a part of it, and right, wrong, or indifferent, it's a natural reaction to make assumptions about certain people, situations, or locations.

I vividly remember one day when I was doing a story about high school security. The script I wrote called for an on-camera close up at a school with a football field behind me. Rather than going through the red tape of talking to school authorities and getting permission to go on campus to do the shoot, I decided to stand on the sidewalk next to the school. The entire sequence would take about five minutes, and I'd be out of there. The story itself had nothing to do with the particular school we were using, it was just the background I needed for my story.

Problem is, our mobile unit isn't unobtrusive, and it attracts attention wherever it goes. The twin transmitting dishes, two feet in diameter, sit in plain view atop the unit, attached to masts that can extend thirty feet into the air. There are generator boxes on top, a platform on the roof, twin spotlights, assorted antennae, and an all-white chassis that turns heads when we drive by.

The part of town we were in was well known for its gang activity, and as we pulled up, we could see a half-dozen young men across the street in white T-shirts and jeans staring at us.

Even though gang members are often sullen, hostile, and distant, and blame the reporters for all the negative publicity that gets on the air, they usually won't bother us.

I did my on-camera report two or three times and decided I had what I needed to finish my story. I was standing on the sidewalk going over my notes for the script while my cameraman and sound man collected their gear and carried it to the rear of the truck. With them on the other side of the vehicle, it looked as if I was standing alone on the sidewalk. As I made a few marks in my notebook, out of the corner of my eye, I saw one of the young men slowly walking across the street towards me. I tried not to look nervous, and I didn't want to create any attention by calling out to my crew, so I decided not to give any indication that I noticed his approach.

He stopped for a moment, and I looked up. I felt my heart pounding in my chest. Did he have a gun? Was he going to pay me back for a report I may have done?

He a few steps closer and smiled. "I'm sorry, Mr. Chambers. I didn't want to interrupt you while you were writing, but could I have your autograph?"

Isn't it wonderful when our negative assumptions are proven wrong?

CHAPTER 17

Breaker . . . Breaker . . . Breaker

A news beat is not always filled with action. I had to learn to live with long periods of time when little happens, and it's always a shock to the system when you jump from doing nothing right into the heart-pumping excitement of a fast-breaking story.

A radio scanner is often the only sound I hear during those lonely hours when nothing is going on. Red digital zeros resembling tiny video games run across the narrow screen of the thin scanners sitting on the dashboard of the darkened mobile unit. In reality, they are sophisticated radio systems that monitor hundreds of emergency channels, each moving to its own beep. The zeros disappear when a call is picked up, and new numbers freeze on the selector screen. They mark the radio frequency captured on the searching scanner. When the transmission is finished, the parade of red zeros starts again.

Three of these units sat in front of me. Night after night, I watched the procession of digits and listened to the eclectic selection of calls. I was always looking for that one transmission that might mean a major story was happening in the city. To do this, I had to wade through countless routine broadcasts and conversations while sifting through bits of static, unintelligible voices, and strange digital sounds.

For hours, cameramen Greg Hunter, Jim Toten, and I cruised the city streets listening and waiting, always staying in constant radio communication with the assignment editor in the newsroom who was also listening to a similar bank of radios. Since he was in the center of everything, he could phone the news sources directly and check on reports that might be important, while we, out in the field, concentrated on the scanners.

Now, as then, the assignment editor is the one to give the final word on whether to go on a breaking news story or not. The most important question is: What will be going on when we get there? It's the essence of a breaking story. Take a fire, for example. How far away is it? Will there be anything to shoot when we arrive? If it's a single-family residential home, chances are that the fire will be out and the firemen will have cleaned up and be ready to leave the scene by the time we get there. The big fires are often the easy ones, and we know they'll still be burning when we arrive . . . except when they aren't. In short, there is no set answer on whether to go or not, so intuition plays a big part in the decision.

The best advice given to me about covering a breaking story was: When in doubt, go. There's nothing worse than holding back and listening to the emergency radios go on and on about the problems they're facing. The decision is subjective, and you can of course be wrong. However, the worst thing for an assignment editor or a news crew is knowing about a story and not going. The pain of seeing it on another news channel that night is unbearable.

Talking about a breaker and being in on one are two different things. When we are in the middle of breaking news, we know what real pressure is, and it's all played out against time. We battle traffic, try to talk our way through police roadblocks, squint at a map that's impossible to read, and listen to voices that shriek over the radio. We become swept up in a rising emotional tide as we get closer to the scene. When we get our camera gear and jump out of the truck, everything is on automatic. There is no time to think it out, and we're carried away by the storm.

I've been through hundreds of breaking stories. I remember one night in 1979 when our crew was racing back on the Hollywood Freeway from a murder scene in Westlake in Ventura County. I was sitting in the bumpy front seat of our mobile unit, scribbling my copy in a reporter's notebook. Cameraman Dave Moore was driving while engineer John Fischer sat in the back. Although the deadline for our ten o'clock newscast was close, I didn't feel too much pressure because I knew we'd get back about an hour before airtime. My report was finished, and I sat ready to record the soundtrack in the front seat the moment we pulled up to the newsroom door. This would give a writer enough time to edit my report on the shooting and schedule it for the early part of the newscast.

As we drove down Van Ness, Akila Gibbs on the assignment desk radioed us. "Unit Two, where are you now?"

Dave picked up the radio and answered her. "We're off the freeway and just about to come on the lot."

"There's been an accident on the Golden State Freeway. Stand by," she said before abruptly cutting off.

I'd noticed the tension in her voice. "It might be big," I said. "Think we have time to cover it?"

We kept on driving to the station, past the on-ramp that would have taken us to the Golden State Freeway. Here came every journalist's nightmare predicament: If we covered the accident on the Golden State Freeway, we would lose the Westlake murder story. If we waited, we might be too late to cover the freeway accident.

We turned into the main gate at KTLA and waved to the security guard. Dave Moore whirled the truck toward the newsroom and sped to our parking place at the far end of the lot. John Fischer, our sound man, jumped out and ran to the back of the unit, grabbed a cassette, and shoved it into his videotape recorder. I turned on my gooseneck light so I could read the copy I had scrawled in my notebook. If we could record the sound track in the next minute or so, we could finish the murder story and still get to the traffic accident.

Suddenly, we heard Akila's voice. This time, it was high pitched and nervous. "They are calling five rescue ambulances to the Golden State Freeway. You'd better go."

"Have someone come outside to the truck so we can give you the murder story," Dave said.

I nodded, held my copy up to the light, and John said, "Go in five seconds."

I turned off the various radios as John let the tape run for a few seconds before I started to record the audio track.

Our chief news engineer, Jeff Webreck, came running out for the tape. He started to open the door but stopped when he saw we were recording and waited until I finished. "I'll take the tapes," he shouted. "See you later." He slammed the door as Dave jammed his foot on the accelerator, and we were off.

"News, this is Unit 2," Dave called into the mike, as we careened out of the gate.

"Go ahead, Unit 2," Akila answered.

"Can you find out exactly where the accident is? Is it northbound, southbound, on the transition road? It'll help us get there faster if we know exactly where it is."

"Northbound." She paused. "Did you read that? Northbound."

"Yeah, we got that," Dave turned the corner at Sunset Boulevard and roared up toward Western.

"It's on the northbound Golden State Freeway, just before the transition road to the Ventura. The California Highway Patrol has confirmed one fatality and four injuries.... There are five ambulances at the scene."

"We're on our way," Dave answered, as he weaved through the traffic to Los Feliz. He would pick up the Golden State Freeway near Griffith Park.

My radios were quiet. Although I was getting some transmissions on my fire channels, I wasn't able to get more information than what Akila had given us. We drove past the Griffith Park entrance and looked down to the freeway to see if traffic had completely stopped.

"Are there emergency shoulders on the Golden State?" Dave asked, as he looked at the long parade of stationary red taillights from the cars heading northbound toward the accident scene.

"I think there are," John Fischer said from the darkness of the back seat.

"Want to try it?" Dave asked as he looked for a place to whip around and squeeze onto the freeway on-ramp.

"It's about all we can do," I answered.

Dave eased past the cars waiting to enter the jammed northbound freeway. The accident was about a mile and a half ahead, and traffic was at a standstill. It looked like we were trapped. Dave worked our mobile unit over to the far right side and moved slowly behind the line of big trucks.

"Why don't you get on the shoulder?" John said.

"It's too narrow, I don't think we can get through," he said. "Although. . . "

A high wall bordered the emergency lane at the far right side of the freeway. Dave pulled onto the narrow shoulder and moved slowly past the stalled traffic. It was so narrow that at one point he scraped his outside mirror on the side of the wall. Trucks on our left and the wall on our right hid our view of what was up ahead.

Finally we reached the flashing red lights. Several officers from the Highway Patrol were busy waving drivers over to the far right lane. The rest of the freeway was completely shut down. Up ahead, dozens more red and blue lights flashed and smoking red flares highlighted the emergency workers, who were everywhere.

It was just moments before the ten o'clock news would be going on the air. John took a quick survey of the scene and realized that by sending a live signal to our transmitter on Mount Wilson, we could televise from here, right in the middle of the freeway.

Dave and John opened the back end of the truck, pulled their gear out, and ran toward the accident while plugging the video cable from the tape recorder into the camera. Dave balanced his light belt on his shoulder and prepared to start shooting the moment they reached the lighted area.

I ran ahead to get what information I could for the live cut-in. Mike Meadows from the *Los Angeles Times* stood nearby with cameras hanging around his neck. "Stan, it's a head-on," he said breathlessly. "A wrong-way driver. The other car was filled with people. A dead man is still pinned in there. The others are being treated."

The paramedics and firemen performed their long-rehearsed dance with precision as they treated the victims on the side of the freeway and used the Jaws of Life to pry one man from the car. Showers of flying sparks erupted from the spinning edge of a screeching, grinding saw-wheel as they cut into the metal of the twisted wreckage.

Mike took countless pictures of the firemen swarming around the scene as he explained the situation to me. "The CHP got word that there was a wrong-way driver on the Ventura Freeway about ten or fifteen minutes before this happened. They did everything they could to flag down the driver, but no such luck. Here's where it ended."

"Drunk?" I asked.

"No," Mike answered, "Some older lady, disoriented or something. She got on going the wrong way and has been driving about fifty miles an hour all this time, barely missing all the oncoming cars. She finally smashed into this one."

Dave and John videotaped the scene for our news report. They had dramatic action shots of the paramedics trying to help the badly injured victims still lying on the freeway roadway. When they finished, Dave ran back to get more cable for our transmission. He lay nearly three hundred feet of cable to connect the transmitting truck to his camera. John was back at the truck making final tests to ensure our picture was getting to the transmitter and that we were ready to go on the air live.

I was getting last minute details from a CHP sergeant and a fire chief when Dave shouted at me. "Stan! We're ready to go!"

The newscast back at KTLA had just begun, and I could hear anchorman Hal Fishman's voice in my earphone, along with the director in the studio, the engineer in the news center, and John Fischer in our remote unit at the scene.

"We're ready to go," I said, calmly, into my microphone.

I watched the splash of colors from the rescue workers, police cars, fire engines, and ambulances as they darted about the freeway in a desperate struggle to tend to the victims. I stood, still waiting for the cue, but none came. I spoke with a bit more urgency. "Tell the director we're ready and should go right away. This is very important."

I got the sudden feeling no one was listening to us back at the studio. Here was a tragic story going on before our eyes and the studio hadn't cut to us. My frustration rose. What was going on? Had they heard us back there? Did they understand the urgency of this report? Again, I told several people that I knew were on the line to relay my request to the director and to Gerry Ruben, the producer. I knew if they realized what a big story we had they would go to us right away, no matter what was happening at the studio. I kept insisting over the communication line, "Studio, tell them to take us. Now!"

Finally someone responded: "They are not going to do it right away."

"Tell Gerry," I insisted.

"They know all about what you have there, and they're not going to take it. Now, damn it, get off the line and keep quiet."

"I won't get off the line. *You* get off the line. Tell the director to take us now," I shouted. Who was he kidding? We'd fought hard to get to this story in order to let people know what was going on, and now I was being told it wouldn't be aired?

Tempers smoked across the line, and I could see this tragic story evaporating before my eyes. Two ambulances had already left the scene, and the initial sense of being at the center of a breaking story was slipping away.

Finally a voice of reason came on the line. "Okay, Stan, we heard your last call. We are going to come to you in thirty seconds."

Thankfully, Dave Moore kept on shooting, and he had sent many dramatic pictures back to the studio during the long delay, which could now be used in our live report.

"Fifteen seconds."

The rescue teams were on the roadway next to me, working on one of the seriously injured victims, as I stood next to the two cars that had crashed head-on. Firemen were putting out the last of the flames and beginning the mop up operations.

"Five seconds. . . . You're on!"

We did an extended live report and used videotape of the action from before we went on the air. However, it wasn't what it could have been. This is a prime example of some of the frustrations involved whenever you try to go live.

Even though ours is a communications business, communication can be one of our biggest problems, oddly enough. I couldn't convey the urgency of the story to our producer, and, as such, he had no idea of the magnitude of what we were covering. The number of people between his earphone and my microphone blurred our communications. He told me later that had he known we were on the verge of losing our visuals, he would have cut to us right away.

In short, no one was to blame. It was just another example of the possible snafus that can befall a live report. There are so many things that can happen to knock you off the air, but the feeling of accomplishment when things go well more than makes up for it.

CHAPTER 18
The Malibu Fire of 1970

It was like a river of fire was flowing across the dry Malibu hills, leaping from tree to tree and exploding as it consumed each one into a cyclonic funnel of black smoke. The heat was so intense that vast acres of dry brush far downhill from the flames erupted at once, making a violent, hissing roar as flames rolled down the hillside, incinerating everything in their path. Devil winds whipped the blazing canyons and hills as the firestorm destroyed everything it touched.

The Telemobile was across the deepest canyon from the fires, the winds whipping it toward the sea. Firemen at the command post said there was no way it could be stopped until it hit the ocean, many miles ahead. Although we saw the destruction and felt the searing heat, we couldn't take pictures from our location. In 1970 we didn't carry film cameras on the Telemobile, and we had no videotape recorders small enough to fit into a mobile unit. Before we could get on the air and show the fire, we had to find a high peak where we could both see the flames and send a live signal to our transmitter on Mount Wilson. That meant getting ahead of the fire. The road we were on was no place for a mobile unit, since a simple shift in the direction of the wind could send the fire racing across the valley toward us.

I took a close look at my map and saw a road several miles ahead that could take us to the other side of a towering mountain, to a communications center atop one of the highest peaks. This would get us ahead of the fire and put us high enough that we could get a signal out to Mount Wilson.

The narrow road and hairpin turns wound all the way up the mountain and took us away from the towering smoke clouds. It was a different world up there. The heavily wooded Malibu countryside was wild but serene. The only sign of fire was the black cloud miles away.

We talked with people who appeared concerned about the fire, but the general consensus was that it was too far away to be a real threat. Since there weren't many escape routes if the fire changed directions and overran their homes, nearly all the residents were outside, keeping a close eye on the ominous smoke cloud.

We entered the empty parking lot of the communications center and drove through the open chain link gate to the highest point. There was nothing on the peak other than four stucco buildings and a long concrete structure with a dozen or so communication dishes on the roof. We weren't worried because the wide parking area would provide ample protection if the flames started to climb the mountainside.

The three of us jumped out of the Telemobile into the buffeting wind to begin our broadcast. Roger climbed the ladder on the back of the truck and pulled up the pipe that supported our transmitting dish. He extended the mast to its thirty-foot-high limit and tried to aim the dish at Mount Wilson. The wind kept rocking it back and forth, and he fought to get a clear signal. Meanwhile, Rich was on the radio talking to the engineers on Mount Wilson.

There was the crackle of cross talk on the radio. "I see your picture, Telemobile. Can you pan it slowly?"

"This wind is something else," Rich answered. He leaned out the window and shouted up to Roger, "Pan it to the left."

"I'll try," Roger yelled back. "This whole truck is jumping in the wind."

"They have our signal. The panning might make it a little clearer," Rich shouted.

"I know, I know," Roger mumbled, as he manually turned the pipe a little to the left while the dish waved precariously in the wind.

"Don't make too big a deal out of it," the engineer from Mount Wilson said. "The signal is pretty good. Why don't you just lock it in? We'll go with what you have."

Roger tightened the clamp and came down the ladder. The truck door barely opened in the gusting wind, and he forced his way into the truck. Above our heads, the transmitting dish and the mast holding it continued to bounce and wave in the wind. We all kept our fingers crossed that everything would hold.

"Amazing. The signal is strong," Rich said as he looked at the monitor.

"Great. Let's get the camera and cable out," Roger said as he prepared to go back out into the windstorm.

I told the newsroom we had a complete view of the mountains, and all we had to do was wait for the fire. The newsroom was in no hurry; they were pleased that we'd found a point where we could get a signal out.

We kept an eye on the black cloud in the distance. It seemed to be growing bigger, but no flames were visible. Waiting can be mind-numbing, and we spent the time wondering if we'd made the wrong decision or picked a bad spot. Maybe we should have stayed with the fire and at least tried to get a signal out, or maybe we should have tried a closer hilltop. Our doubts grew stronger the longer we waited.

A sheriff's car with its red lights flashing paused at the open gate and drove up the rest of the hill to our unit. "Where did you guys come from?" he asked as he got out. He was wearing goggles and heavy gloves.

"We had to find a good spot to get our television picture out," I said. "We saw plenty of fire below, but we couldn't get a signal out."

"How long before you can get out of here?"

"Oh, we're staying," I called back. "We're going to get some great shots. That fire was really going when we saw it down in the canyon."

"I know it is, and it is coming right this way. I've been told to get you out of here."

"That's okay, Sheriff," I answered as we walked toward each other. "We'll be all right. This is the only place we can get our picture out."

"I'm sorry, but you can't stay here."

"I understand your concern," I insisted, "but we'll be all right. There's plenty of flat area up here. The parking section alone will hold back any flames. Don't worry about us."

"Look, when those flames race up this peak on all sides, it's going to be like a blast furnace. Everything is going to go. I don't care about your television signal. I'm not going to let you guys stay."

"Sheriff, this is our job. You worry about those people below. We'll take care of ourselves."

"They're all gone below. I came up here to make sure there weren't any phone company engineers still here. I've got some other people to check on. Will you cooperate with me and get out of here?"

There were still no flames visible, and the place looked perfectly safe to me. I wasn't about to leave, and I think the sheriff could tell.

He got back into his patrol car. "Look, I have to check a ranch on the ocean side of the mountain. I'll be back in ten minutes, and I want you out of here." He backed up and rode a small dust cloud to the gate.

"Just our luck to get a guy like that at a time a time like this," Roger said, as we watched the flashing red lights disappear down the winding road.

I walked back to our truck. "He'll be back."

As we reached the Telemobile, I saw the first flames work their way over a distant ridge below.

"Hello, newsroom, this is the Telemobile, checking in. What's the latest from your end?"

"We hoped you would have the latest, Telemobile."

"Well, just as I'm talking, I can see some flames coming up over a hill. They're still pretty far away, but unless the winds change, they should be coming our way. I haven't got any idea how long it will take."

"Give us a mark on your location again."

"It's the communications peak . . . the very top. I'm not sure, but we might get some pretty terrific shots here in a while."

"That communications peak is right in the path of the fire. At least that's what the command post is saying. It's going to the sea, and you're right in its path."

For some insane reason, I still didn't see the reason for too much concern. "You know how those estimates are—it goes in the general direction, but it doesn't necessarily mean it's going to burn everything. Besides, we have a big flat spot . . . a good-sized parking lot here. Even if the flames come close, we'll be all right."

"Well, I hope so," the newsroom voice shot back. "When can we do a live spot?"

"We're ready when you are. I can do a spot right now. The flames are still far away, but the smoke is black and it looks huge over the hills."

"Can you be ready in ten minutes?"

"We're ready now."

Just as we completed our live report, we could see the dust of the sheriff's car tearing up the road. Roger stood in front of the Telemobile. "What are we going to do?"

"Let's check the desk," I said.

"Telemobile, good job on the live report," the newsroom said. "That black cloud certainly looks ominous."

"Not as ominous as the sheriff coming up the hill," I called back. "Is it too dangerous for us to stay?"

"That's what the deputy says."

"The wire copy says they are evacuating everyone from there. What are you going to do?" the voice over the radio asked.

"We're staying," I paused a moment. "Unless you say differently."

"Let me talk to the others in the newsroom," he answered.

After a long wait I asked, "Newsroom, why don't we just wait a while longer before making any final decisions?"

There was no response.

Roger called up from the front of the truck, "I can see the flames now; they're coming up over the ridge. They're huge."

I studied them for a moment, then pushed the transmit button on the microphone. "News, I'm getting off the radio for a moment. The sheriff just arrived."

The deputy slammed on his brakes, and ran over to us. "Look, I told you to get out of here. I don't want to waste any more time. Those flames will be here any minute. Now get out of here!" He was infuriated. "I've gotten everyone else out. I'm not going to be responsible for you guys killing yourselves."

"Let me talk to the newsroom," I answered.

"You're not talking to anyone. You're getting out."

I walked back to the front seat and put the radio mike up to my mouth. "He's back and he's giving me real heat."

"Telemobile, this is news," the voice replied. "We've just checked with top management and the word is to get out of there. They don't want you guys getting hurt or taking any chance of losing the Telemobile."

The sheriff was adamant. "Get out or I'll arrest you."

Having gotten my answer from the newsroom, I was satisfied it was time to go. "We'll follow you down the hill."

Dust clouds stirred up by our vehicles were whipped high into the air by the fierce wind as we wound our way down the mountaintop to Pacific Coast Highway. There, we waited for the flames to reach the ocean. We did several live shots that night as the flames rolled over the mountains and exploded in the dry brush on the ocean side of the hills. In most cases, even though the black, choking smoke was only six feet off the ground, the firemen used Pacific Coast Highway as a fire break and held back the spreading flames from reaching the beach homes below. Despite everything they did, several beach homes were lost.

We drove back to the communications peak the next day, after the fire had run its course. On our way up to the peak, we saw homes and ranches that had been reduced to burned-out skeletons. The Malibu hills were barren, covered with layers of powdery gray ash. We retraced our steps to our mountaintop perch from the previous day. All the brush was gone, and all the trees had burned.

The fire had roared through the entire mountain. Yet the spot where we had parked was untouched. Since it was the highest point on the peak, the parking lot had protected it from the onslaught of the flames, and that particular area was as pristine as when we had done our reports the day before.

Even though that spot had come through unscathed, I don't know how we would have fared. What would the intense heat have done to the Telemobile and its oxygen-starved crew huddled inside? Would we have survived? I felt uncertain as I stood there surrounded by the vast acreage of lonely ashen land, and I silently thanked the sheriff for standing up to this hard-headed journalist.

Behind the Scenes

So much of what I go through never gets on the air. I cover the story. My cameraman shoots the videotape and captures the visual elements to show the viewer what happened. I write the narration and explain the facts as best I can. The finished report goes on the air and the viewer gets a sense of what took place. But, like the Malibu brush fire, so many things happen that can never be experienced by anyone who wasn't at the scene. It's a case of, "You really had to be there."

One of the best stories that I wish had made it to the air centered around my friend Eli Ressler, who was the consummate professional cameraman. His basic assignment was to be on the spot wherever news was happening in the city, so he always kept his small, handheld sixteen-millimeter Bell and Howell at his side.

Eli was driving on the Santa Monica Freeway one hot August day when the assignment editor called him on the car radio. "Eli, we have a copter on the pad at Santa Monica Airport. A big brush fire just broke out in the Malibu hills, one of many that threaten this seaside community. Structures are threatened."

"I'm on my way," Eli said. "Is Wally Smith the pilot?" he asked.

"No, Wally is too far away. I'm not sure who the pilot is, but the copter is waiting for you."

Eli was no more than five minutes away. When he wheeled into the airport, he pulled into a space by the security shack, grabbed his camera, and raced to the noisy helicopter. Ducking his head as he ran under the spinning blades, Eli jumped into the passenger seat, quickly shut the door, and buckled the safety straps over his shoulders and around his waist.

"Let's go along the coast to Malibu," he shouted over the roar of the engine. The young-looking pilot looked at him for a moment, nodded his head and took off.

A black, billowing cloud loomed over the mountains as they left the ground. Neither man spoke as they flew toward the fire. Eli kept checking his camera, putting in new film, and cleaning the lens while trying mentally to push the copter toward the fire. "Go in low, keep the sun behind us, and stay out of the smoke," Eli yelled. The hesitant pilot responded with a nervous look and a nod.

It was a shaky pass, too high to get any good shots. Eli ordered the pilot to go around and do it again. The second pass was much better, if maybe a little too close. The pilot was a bit unsteady, but the shots were dramatic. Eli was pleased, but he wanted to be sure he had enough footage, so he had his pilot make a half dozen more passes before waving him off and telling him to return to the airport. He noticed perspiration running down the pilot's taut face as the copter headed back toward Santa Monica. He looked a little too nervous for comfort.

"What's the matter, haven't you ever flown with a news cameraman before?" Eli shouted over the engine noise.

The pilot turned toward him with a pained expression, and whispered, "Aren't you my new flight instructor?"

The story of Eli's flight is one of the best descriptions of what it is like being in television news. It captures the blows, the encounters, and the surprises any one of us might face every day. Learning to live with them is the only way to survive in television news.

"Expect the unexpected," is one of the best phrases to describe Eli's adventure, as well as the volatility of the news business. If a reporter understands that anything can happen, he's more apt to derive pleasure in the countless situations he'll invariably stumble upon in the news world. I believe the unexpected is the main catalyst that helps me thoroughly enjoy my day-to-day work as a reporter.

Eli was momentarily startled when he realized his precarious position in doing a dangerous report with an inexperienced pilot. But by the time he slammed his car door and headed back to the studio, he'd forgotten his copter adventure and was concentrating on getting the brush fire footage back before the broadcast deadline.

While Eli's adventure would have made a great story on the ten o'clock news, I'm sure he subtracted years off that pilot's life.

CHAPTER 19
The Eighties: The Pressure Cooker

The eighties began with an inflationary recession and bounced into an economic boom. In business, there were mega-mergers, junk bonds, and failed savings and loans. Terrorists hijacked ships, downed passenger jets, and shot up churches. Drug cartels made headlines as cocaine and heroin flooded the country and inner city gangs fought over the drug trade.

Iran and Iraq fought a vicious, bloody war. The Middle East continued to be rocked by violence. And the United States agonized over revolutions in El Salvador and Nicaragua, and planned a "Star Wars" defense against the communists.

There were assassination attempts on President Ronald Reagan and Pope John Paul II. President Anwar Sadat of Egypt was killed by assassins. Mikhail Gorbachev and Ronald Reagan began their series of historic meetings that brought the Cold War to an end. It was a fast-paced time, and the idea of, "You snooze, you lose" was never more apt. That included our broadcasts.

I had met Ronald Reagan several times while he was governor of California, but the meeting I remember the most was in early 1980, before he officially started campaigning for the Republican nomination. I was at the Los Angeles International Airport covering the arrival of President Carter during the Iranian hostage situation. Persian students were still holding Americans at the US Embassy in Tehran, and the situation was getting worse. President Carter made a brief statement at the airport before he departed.

I whisked the videotape back to our Telemobile and drove it to the spot on the other side of the airport where we could transmit to our newsroom for broadcast. Not only was this a great place for our transmission, but it also happened to be the area where VIPs are given special escorts to their planes. It was dark, and I was waiting in front of the camera when I saw a black Cadillac pull up. As I stood in the glare of the television lights, I could see a man walking over to our truck.

He waved a greeting. "Hi Stan, what's the big news tonight?" It was Barney, Ronald Reagan's bodyguard and driver when he was governor of California. I hadn't seen him for years.

We exchanged greetings and talked a little. "What brings you out here, Barney?"

"I brought the governor here to catch a plane."

"Reagan? You mean Reagan's here?"

"Over in the car. His plane leaves pretty soon."

"Do you think there's a chance I could interview him about the hostage situation?" I asked.

"Why not? I'll ask him."

I told the station to stand by, that I might have live footage of Reagan's reaction to Carter's statement.

"Ronald Reagan live?" was their surprised reply.

"He'll be right over, Stan," Barney called back. "Are you ready now?"

"Can we go right away?" I asked the director over my microphone.

"We're ready when you are," came the answer.

We kept our camera on top of the Telemobile in those days. With it up there, we would always be ready to go on the air when we arrived at a story. Since the camera was so high off the ground, the engineers had built a platform on the front bumper to bring reporters and their interviews up to the level of the camera. This was how they eliminated the unflattering downward angle and were able to shoot the reporters head-on. However, it was a high step up to the platform.

"Governor, do you mind stepping up here?" I asked.

It was a higher step than Mr. Reagan expected. His knee hit the base of the platform as he pulled himself up. His expression told me that it had really hurt.

"I'm fine," he said, as he straightened himself up and prepared for the interview.

Afterwards, as he said goodbye and stepped down from the high platform, I could see a slight limp as he walked back to his car. How I worried about that misstep. I was afraid I'd almost stopped his campaign before it officially started. No one was more grateful than when he got back to the car. Whenever I noticed that slight limp in later years, I always wondered if it had been caused by that night at the Los Angeles International Airport.

Being in Two Places At Once

There were so many times when I needed to be in two places at the same time. One of those instances happened while we were doing a report from what had once been John Wayne's yacht. The former minesweeper, converted to a thing of beauty, graced the Newport Harbor for twenty-five years before Wayne sold it to Lynn Hutchins, a wealthy lawyer. In 1983, Lynn now had it up for sale for two million dollars, and our news crew clamored aboard to do a story on the sale.

As I entered the wheelhouse, I couldn't help but notice pictures and memorabilia belonging to John Wayne on the bulkhead. "Wayne wouldn't have approved of all these pictures," Lynn said. "But they add so much to the feeling of the boat that I put them up anyway."

He gave me a brief tour of the grand salon while Dave Moore, my cameraman, wandered around, videotaping the boat. "John Wayne carefully screened me before he sold me the *Wild Goose*," Lynn said as we walked to the deck. "I'm going to be just as careful when I sell it. I'd love to keep it, but my law practice keeps me too busy."

Before I could comment, Dave and sound man Ray Lopez joined us. "We've finished all the shooting. This should make a good story. Are you ready for the interview?" Dave asked.

"Shall we do it here by the wheelhouse?" I asked.

"It's as good place as any. Can both of you get a little closer to the rail?" Dave motioned us over.

Beep . . . Beep . . . Beep . . . My radio pager went off, just as we were getting ready to start. I fumbled with the small beeper and placed it next to my ear. "Go immediately to your truck," the crackling voice on the page ordered. "We have a breaking story."

If I didn't get the interview, the entire story was lost. The main thrust of the news story was Hutchins selling the yacht, and we had yet to film the interview. "Dave, we've got to do this interview quickly," I told him.

Dave agreed, and we taped a brief interview with the owner so we wouldn't walk away empty handed. We picked up our scattered gear from the deck, grabbed our light stands, cables, and extension cords and made a hasty retreat down the gangplank. I yelled back a "Thank you" to our host as we jogged to our camera truck. I knew we had made the right decision.

We contacted our assignment editor as we drove away from the dock. "Go to Torrance Airport, and call me on a land line from there," he ordered. "Pick up some sandwiches if you can; you may not have a chance to eat for some time."

"Sounds pretty big," Dave said, "I'll put on KFWB and see what's brewing."

Because most television stations can listen to each other's radio frequency, our assignment editor didn't always give us specifics of what we were covering or where we were going, assuming we could figure it out on the way by listening to other news stations. Using a pay phone instead of our radios was one way to insure that our conversation would remain out of earshot from our competitors.

KFWB was in the middle of a brief report about an earthquake that had hit the little town of Coalinga in central California. With a perceptive glance at one another, we suddenly knew where we were going.

As we made our way through the rush-hour traffic, we tried to find out as many details as possible from the radio report. Information was still sketchy: a major quake, 6.5 on the Richter scale, the epicenter five miles northwest of Coalinga. They reported severe damage to several brick buildings in the downtown business district, injuries, damage to the local hospital, a number of fires, and downed telephone lines throughout the town.

By the time we reached the airport, everyone in the news business was aware of the magnitude of the damage, and there was no longer any need to avoid using the radio.

"A brown and white twin Cessna, No. 467N, will meet you at Torrance Airport," barked our assignment editor, Scott Barer. "Load up and meet me at Tiger Air at Burbank Airport. I'll have the rest of the gear we'll need for the trip. Finish the John Wayne story on the way, and I'll have a messenger pick it up."

As we drove, I added notes in my notebook, "Coalinga is in Fresno County, about fifty miles from Fresno. It is a small town of about seven thousand, surrounded by farming land and oil fields."

After the brief flight from Torrance to Burbank, we met Scott at Tiger Air Terminal where he loaded additional batteries, chargers, and the backup equipment in case of technical problems. We were airborne about two hours after the quake hit Coalinga. I remember thinking that our luck hadn't abandoned us; we'd gotten the John Wayne story, and the station was doing everything to get us on the Coalinga scene as quickly as possible. But sometimes luck can be a fickle mistress.

We were still over Los Angeles when our first problem arose. The pilot turned to us and gave it to us straight. "Coalinga Airport has been closed down. No one is allowed in but emergency planes. They specifically say that news planes must stay out."

Scott Barer came unglued. "What? They can't do that!" He picked up his handheld radio and relayed the information to the station. "Get the FAA," he called out to the editor in Los Angeles. "I know they just can't close it down."

"I can hear other planes requesting permission to land at Coalinga, too," the pilot said. "The airport is saying no."

In between the urgent requests to get us permission to land at Coalinga, the station gave me the latest update on conditions there. There had been another big earthquake, this one also measuring 6.5

on the Richter scale. I listened and scribbled in my notebook: "Oil field pipe lines have broken and there are some fires, about fifty injured. Some are serious, but no fatalities at this point. At least a dozen old brick buildings in the center of town have been badly damaged. All telephone service is out. The emergency hospital is damaged, no patients can be taken there."

"Studio, see if we can land at Harris Ranch," Scott said. "It's a small strip, but is not too far away from Coalinga."

Our pilot shook his head. "Harris Ranch is also restricted."

"What are they suggesting we do?" Scott asked.

"Land at Hanford, about fifty miles from Coalinga."

Scott was beside himself. "We would never get to the quake scene in time for the broadcast at ten."

"I can hear some of the other stations on the radio, and it appears they're heading for Hanford," the pilot said.

Scott had his handheld radio close to his mouth. "Studio, if you can hear me, get us a rental car and have a cab pick us up at Hanford Airport." No answer. We'd flown too far from Los Angeles, and radio communication with the station was gone. We had no idea if they heard our last transmission or not.

Our luck had deserted us, and our hope of getting a live report from the scene was slithering away. Nothing more could be done but exercise damage control. If we couldn't go live, what could we do instead? I decided to try some telephone reports. If I could find a working phone, the station could show videotape from our news service that should be in the studio in time for the broadcast. They could use my audio report over the pictures.

A big orange sun was setting as we began our descent into Hanford Airport. All of us knew our chances of getting a signal out of the earthquake zone was next to nothing. It would take us an hour to drive there, shoot the damage, and then get a picture out to KTLA via a local television station. But we *had* to get this story on our ten o'clock news.

A cab pulled up next to our plane as we started to unload our gear. "You fellows from KTLA, Los Angeles?"

Yes! The radio call to the station had gotten through. Maybe our luck was changing.

We grabbed our gear and crammed into an old car that had definitely seen better days. While racing to Coalinga, I replayed my last conversation with the studio in my head. They'd liked the idea of my calling in a live report from Coalinga, and the engineers were in the process of rerouting the phone to get my recording on tape so that it could be played back on the news broadcast. To do that, I needed to find a working phone; no easy feat considering that all the lines were supposedly down. Hal Fishman was going to set up the full quake story on the newscast and wanted to talk to me live.

Except for the lights emanating from emergency vehicles and hastily erected floodlights, the city was blacked out as we crept down the main street. Police were worried about looters and had set up roadblocks to keep people from entering the city. We were directed to the command post near the center of town, the area that had suffered the most devastation. No one was allowed to go into the downtown area alone, and we newsmen were required to have a police escort at all times.

We did a double check of our handheld radios and split up. The camera crew waited for their turn to be taken downtown, and I started searching for a working telephone for my opening report on the broadcast. I kept asking if any phones were working and kept getting the same answer; "No, they're all out. No light, power, gas, or phones."

Several people had heard of working phones here and there, and I ran through blocks of rubble and darkness to check them out. Nothing. The manager of a damaged motel heard that some of the phones were working at the shopping center a few blocks away. As I ran to the shopping center, skirting around debris littering the sidewalks and streets, I passed tilting houses, jarred off their foundations, and toppled chimneys. Turning the corner, I came upon a heavenly sight: a shopping center with its lights on and a bank of phones! People were lined up six deep waiting for their turn. I knew I would never make my call to Los Angeles if I had to wait for all of them.

I explained my problem to those standing in line, hoping they'd take pity on this poor newsman. Through their good graces, I was able to work my way up to third in line. I looked at my watch. My hopes of getting through were fading with each minute.

An NBC reporter was on one line talking to her desk in Los Angeles. A wire service reporter was thumbing through his notebook as he talked on the center phone. A man was dialing over and over again, trying to get a working line on the third phone. Another reporter from Bakersfield was standing impatiently, frustrated to be fifth in another line. What we would have given for the advent of cell phones.

The lines worked intermittently, and my efforts to get through were unsuccessful as I stuck the dime in time after time, dialed, got nothing, and tried again. By this time, I was vacillating between wanting to punch the phone in frustration and laughing at my predicament. I knew I should be with the crew in the quake damage area. Viewers expect their television newsmen to be in the middle of the story, not blocks away grinding their teeth over a phone line.

Meanwhile, Scott called me on the radio. "Stan, we're inside. The damage is unbelievable. Any luck on your call?"

"I'm dialing, but nothing is happening." I kept dialing. "Is it worse than you'd expected?"

"Every building I see is badly damaged. Skip loaders are working the debris, and they're still looking for trapped people. No fatalities yet, though."

I continued dialing as he talked, but it was the same story. A dial tone . . . the beep of the buttons . . . a pause . . . a busy signal . . . nothing. I'd already missed my live report at the top of the news, and the station would have to use the tape from an earlier call I'd made from a fast-food store. As the minutes slipped by, I knew my chances of getting in a report before the end of the broadcast were slim.

Suddenly, at 9:50, a voice came on the line. I had reached the studio. During the next commercial, the station put some of the videotape of the damage on standby, and Hal Fishman came on the phone.

The broadcast went well and carried no hint of everything we'd gone through to get the report on the air. Ours was one of the first live reports in Los Angeles. We'd done it. In spite of racing to the scene at breakneck speed, the near hits, and biting frustration, we'd survived another run-in with the pressure cooker and come out on top.

Hal Fishman 1931–2007

I would be remiss if I didn't make a special mention of my good friend Hal Fishman, and how his role as anchor of *News At Ten* since the mid-sixties enhanced our ability to survive all the insanity of reporting the news. In a business where news ratings can dip and disappear overnight, and new anchors move in and out with the regularity of a television commercial, it seems as if Hal was always there.

News is a perishable commodity. It is written on the wind and is consumed by the broadcast each day. The only constant, the main continuity for the viewer, is the man at the anchor desk. He is the familiar figure who is there each night, the one who ties everything together to make sense out of the news scene.

Hal was an exceptional broadcaster, the steady force who was integral in making *News At Ten* a successful local news program. He was more than a newsman; he was an information center with a photographic memory.

Hal anchored much of KTLA's marathon coverage of the Watts riots in the summer of 1965, and his ability to interpret the events and separate fact from fiction did much to forestall the wild rumors running rampant through the city.

When the news of the assassination attempt on Pope John Paul II hit the wires and details were sketchy, Hal was live on the air with the first information. Producer Gerry Ruben called out to Hal,

"Just ad-lib about the Pope for about five minutes while we get more details." Hal did just that, without any change of pace in his delivery.

He had the instinct to say the right thing at the right moment and was never at a loss for words. In October 1993, as the world waited for the jury's verdicts in the riot-connected beating of truck driver Reginald Denny, Hal used that time to discuss legal ramifications and minute details of the law with lawyers and law school deans. His reasoned and reassuring comments helped prepare the viewers for the controversial verdicts.

Hal was one of the major reasons that *News at Ten* became the highest-rated prime time newscast in the history of Los Angeles television. As a tip of the hat to his nearly thirty years at KTLA, Hal received the "Broadcaster of the Year" award from the Society of Professional Journalists in 1994.

On his fortieth year in broadcasting, KTLA named our newsroom the Hal Fishman Newsroom to honor his long years of dedication to the news, and to KTLA. As part of our station's sixtieth anniversary, Hal was again honored at the Autry National Center.

A day after that celebration, my good friend collapsed at home and was rushed to the hospital. Advanced colon cancer was discovered, and Hal passed away on August 7, 2007.

Though someone else sits in his chair now, his presence will always remain in the studio.

CHAPTER 20
The Late Eighties—A Season of Change

The Soviet Union's Curtain Cracks
The summer of 1986 marked the beginning of the end for the USSR. Winds of change blew *glasnost* and *perestroika* across the land, jarring the status quo, and moving the Soviets toward the end of communism. KTLA insisted we should be there to witness it, so I went to Moscow with a small production team, my wife, Beverly, and a wish list of twenty-five news stories we wanted to do while in Moscow.

We were warned on the incoming flight that we weren't permitted to take pictures at the airport. But our producer, Scott Barer, remembered seeing a network news report from Moscow about Pan Am resuming service inside Russia and included the story on our wish list.

Pavel, our official Soviet host, was silent as he scanned our two page list. "I think we will be able to do most of these. However, I'll have to write some letters for permission. It will take some time. Everything takes time in Russia."

"We're not going to be here too long," Scott said. "How long will it take?"

"It all depends," Pavel answered, his eyes moving down the page. "Ah, the Metro is one that will cost some money to do."

We were surprised. "You mean we have to pay to do some of these stories?"

Pavel nodded. "I think they want three hundred rubles to shoot in the Metro."

Scott was visibly shocked. "Three hundred! I never pay to do a story."

Pavel changed the subject as he pointed at the list. "This request to do a story on Moscow's nightlife is a problem. They are very cautious about certain topics. You understand, people don't want to be filmed while they are relaxing. This might be a problem."

We didn't have to wait long for our list to scale down even more.

"Taping at Radio Moscow is also a problem. We don't allow cameras inside. We can probably get an interview with television commentator Vladimir Posner at some other location, but not inside."

Scott held firm. "We were hoping to catch him as he was broadcasting one of his commentaries from his studio at Radio Moscow, then do an interview with him."

"Let me check," Pavel answered with a vague wave of his hand.

By this time, Scott was beginning to wonder if we'd get *any* stories. "What about the story on Pan Am starting up again from Moscow?"

"I don't know about that one. I'll have to ask the civil aviation people."

"Well, if those are going to take some time, why don't we go down to Red Square and do a story there so we can get it back to Los Angeles tomorrow?"

"That takes some time, too," Pavel said.

There was a collective raise of our eyebrows. "What do you mean? It's outside on the street."

"Yes, but we have to get permission to shoot there."

Life here was a series of permissions, privilege, and secrecy, and we wondered how they would take to a freer society. In order to live in the Soviet Union, everyone had credentials. To get into our hotel, the Moskva across from Red Square, we held a death grip on our special passes. Officially, we were told this was to separate us from businesses in the hotel dealing in "hard currency," since many people on the streets wanted to buy jeans, shirts, shoes, anything

American, from tourists. Unofficially, I think they simply wanted to keep a close eye on us. Getting to our room took two checks of our credentials, and the trip to the hotel restaurant earned us another check just for good measure.

In spite of the severity of the rules, the people were a delight, and they took to Beverly like a duck to water. No one was impervious to her charm and friendly smile. The security men smiled and waved or even got up from their seats to greet us when we left the floor. On Beverly's birthday, the woman who cleaned the floor left a vase with four beautiful roses in our room. It was signed from the "collective on the fourth floor."

The manager of Intourist in Moscow went out of his way to meet us in the lobby after we returned from a story that day and called to Beverly, "I want to wish you a happy birthday and hope that you will always remember your visit to Moscow. We will do everything possible to make your stay a happy one." If that wasn't enough, he made hard-to-get dinner reservations for us at the Hotel Berlin, which has subsequently been refurbished into Moscow's premier luxury hotel and renamed The Savoy.

As the days wore on, more of our requests for stories were approved; we got the go-ahead on filming Moscow's nightlife and Radio Moscow. They never did bend on the museums, so we ended up with very few stories, which was a real pity because their rich art and artifacts are breathtaking. The denouement came with the approval of the Pan Am story, and, to this day, it still gives me indigestion to think of how we very nearly missed it.

The deputy chief security officer for Moscow International Airport jumped out of a yellow van that had made a screeching stop on the narrow road bordering the tarmac. Our crew tumbled out and raced across the asphalt into the muddy ruts of wild grass that grew between the road and the airport runways.

The only Pan Am plane scheduled to leave Moscow that day had already taxied the length of the runway, made its final turn, and readied for take off. One of our guys carried a Beta cam, and another carried an extended tripod to steady the camera the moment it was locked on. A third carried a black bag filled with videocassettes and batteries.

Beverly and I stood next to the van, watching our guys race after their shots of the departing plane. The security officer gave us a wide grin while mopping his damp forehead. I thought his smile ironic, considering he was the same person who'd detained us back at the terminal. Here we'd thought he was trying to prevent us from shooting a sensitive security area, when it turned out that he simply couldn't find a van to take us out on the runway.

If we hadn't gotten a videotape of this particular plane, we would have had to scrub our story that focused around the resumption of Pan Am flights between the Soviet Union and the United States. Just as our cameraman bolted the camera onto the tripod and began shooting, the 747 gathered momentum, roared down the runway, and finally lunged into the sky.

I looked over at Beverly, and we shared huge smiles, knowing we'd saved the story by the skin of our teeth. Indeed, times were changing in the Soviet Union.

As my wife and I shared our smiles, I couldn't have possibly known how my own life with her was also about to drastically change.

Beverly

Beverly died on February 4, 1989. She fought cancer for many years after discovering a lump in her breast while we were covering the 1984 Republican Convention. Her operation was a success and we had a few more wonderful years together. The children were mostly grown and busy with their own lives, and this was the first time in our lives that we could enjoy real togetherness.

She moved through the declining stages with great class and patrician dignity up until Thanksgiving, 1988, when she began to fade. Up until then, I drove her to the doctor's office several times a week for her radiation and chemotherapy treatments, where we held hands and talked, trying to ignore the reason for our being there. She was my source of strength with her upbeat attitude, and she never failed to remind me that there was so much more to living than just these treatments.

She was more than my wife and mother to our children. Among countless other things over our decades together, she was my assistant producer at the Democratic Convention in Atlanta and the Republican Convention in New Orleans in the summer of 1988. She was always there to ease the stresses and tensions, and to enjoy the elation when our live broadcasts and reporting went well.

One hot, sticky afternoon in New Orleans will always stand out in my mind. After a delightful lunch in the French Quarter, Beverly suggested we walk down to the Mississippi River bank a few blocks away so she could see President George Bush arrive in New Orleans on the big paddlewheel riverboat. Even though Scott Barer and I had previously agreed to use CNN's feed for our report, Beverly's enthusiasm got the better of us, and we decided to take our crew and shoot it anyway. It turned out to be the best and most visual story we did on the whole convention.

Later that night in the Superdome, I enlisted Beverly's help with a live five-minute cut-in from our skybox above the convention hall. Everything was set up with then-California Senator, and later Governor, Pete Wilson. He had agreed to be a guest on the program, so we made sure to stay in touch with his staff during the days of the convention. It was getting close to airtime and there was no senator. I planted Beverly next to the top escalator so she could eye every person entering the hallway while I returned to the skybox to do the live broadcast. Without the senator, I wracked my brain to figure out how I was going to fill the time.

Access to the skyboxes are through a walkway lined with a series of doors that all look alike. Unless someone in Wilson's party saw Beverly standing outside, they would never be able to find our skybox. We had been so diligent in managing every detail, so it seemed like a cruel joke to have missed the important one; the final assurance that Pete Wilson would be there.

Beverly's assignment was to recognize the senator and bring him immediately to our skybox. Our broadcast began live to Los Angeles, but without Pete Wilson. Beverly was frantic until she saw a group of men moving fast and determinedly.

The first man stopped. Beverly's voice shook with anxiety and trepidation. "Pete?"

"Bev?"

Without another word, she grabbed Pete and ran him to our skybox, where we had a great interview. We celebrated for so long at dinner that night that we closed the restaurant. Victories snatched from certain defeat are the ones we savor the most. To know that Beverly had saved the day made the victory even sweeter. That was typical of my wife. Where we sometimes found a blocked wall for getting an interview, Beverly could always find an opening.

This talent was displayed quite nicely on our trip to Poland and the Vatican in 1987. Our excitement about the trip was tarnished by the recurrence of Beverly's cancer. We seriously considered canceling, but the doctor assured us that it was okay for us to go. The idea of doing a documentary on the Pope—visiting his birthplace, seeing where he lived, going to the rock quarry where he worked, and seeing where he hid out from the Nazis during World War II—was too exciting pass up, and we decided to go. Beverly and I quickly agreed that we couldn't miss our third trip behind the Iron Curtain.

She was a tireless traveler and great sport. I remember how nervous we all were during the turbulent, rocky flight from Rome to Krakow on a Polish LOT airliner. The plane bounced around in the sky while our party of five made periodic checks out the window to make sure the wings were still attached. Meanwhile, all of our suitcases and most of our television gear were driven to Kracow in rented cars.

After an especially severe and unnerving bump, Beverly gamely broke the tension. "Aren't you glad our luggage is safe down there in the cars?"

After landing in Kracow, we joined up with our Polish press officer, who tried to help us find the lodge where the Pope skied while he was bishop of Krakow. We searched the hillside city, and finally he stopped the car and asked a nun walking along the road in her flowing black robes if she had any idea where it was.

"I'll be glad to take you there. That's where I am going," she said. She got into our crowded car and we drove another five minutes to a beautiful building amid the mountains and trees.

The sisters weren't expecting us and told us they couldn't let us in the house until they spoke to their Mother Superior in town. Talk about awkward. Everyone just stood around the patio and looked at each other. Beverly, as always, was quick on her feet, and she broke the ice by pulling out a picture of our eleven children and showing them to the sister in charge. The sister got a good laugh out of it and immediately permitted us to bring our camera equipment inside and shoot the room where the Pope stayed on his ski vacations. Where KTLA's best failed, a lovely woman with eleven children could save the day.

I tried to put my life on automatic pilot after I lost Beverly. I threw myself into work, hoping its demands could stabilize my aimlessness. I came home after my night shift, turned on Ted Koppel and *Nightline*, and fell asleep when it was over. I went to mass every morning, took long walks to a little breakfast place in Larchmont Village, read the morning papers, and topped it off with another long walk home. I began to set a pattern that helped me get through the impossible time.

My biggest concern was for my children, and I was on the phone with them every day. I wanted to thank them again and again for their understanding through the years, about all the missed vacations, skipped dinners, and picnics at the beach without their father; for being so accepting when I couldn't be a manager of their little league teams or go to parent's night at school. Television siphoned away a lot of my time from the family, but it was Beverly who let them know that it was necessary. It was an occupational hazard of being in the news business.

It was a shock to look around and see that my kids were all grown. How could this have happened so fast? Where I had taken care of them, they were now taking care of me and helping me through the endless days of my grief.

My daughter Beverly and her husband Don invited me to spend the weekends at Mission Viejo in Orange County. I always had a ready guest room at Jim and Jane's house at Solano Beach. They took me for long walks along the beach where we watched the yacht races off the pier. Nancy always invited me to lunch at Redondo Beach. Stan, Dave, and Ed were always on the phone to make sure Dad was doing well.

John and Bob helped me with house repairs, doing do all of those nagging things that happen to old homes. Margaret took over the accounting and made sure all my bills were paid every month, even though she was working a full schedule in the intensive care unit of Children's Hospital. Mary was starting a new career in Santa Barbara, and I enjoyed my long weekends up there. Had it been so long ago that Margaret and Mary, not quite in their teens, would come to KTLA and help me put together my Sunday night newscast? They pasted scripts together, framed pictures for the broadcast, and tidied up the newsroom while I wrote my scripts. They often borrowed quarters from my co-anchor, Dick Garton, so they could get snacks out of the food machine.

I remember how my youngest daughter, Elizabeth, helped run our house during those dark days. She was everyone's baby sister and loved it. She is the only one of my kids who went into television news like her dad.

During those long, lonesome walks in the brisk morning air, I often thought about the days when my family was young. It was a rush to breakfast, a hurried carpool to school, signing notes for the teachers, then off to work for me. I remembered how effortlessly Beverly handled everything. She made those years smooth and delightful for our growing family. She always had the right answer to all the kids' questions.

I saw my children become more independent. It was a continuation of my theory of the open hand: keep it open so that the baby can walk and hold your fingers, or let go and be on his own. We must stay close to those we love, even as they go their separate ways. My children's love and their lives through all these turbulent years taught me many things. I am a better, more concerned, understanding, and knowing newsman because of them. They taught me how important it is to keep the human spark glowing when I'm in the middle of a difficult story. I share the anxiety and sorrow, the bewilderment and futility of others when they find themselves trapped in crisis. I am especially vulnerable to their feelings because of the tenderness our family has always shared.

I never had to worry about a generation gap in covering stories because I bridged it every day with my family. My children kept me posted on the trends, the vibrations, and directions they and their friends live through. And when my mosaic of news stories is completed and brought into focus, my family will have added the bright splashes to the mural that makes sense out of it all.

But without Beverly, the lonesome path will always be a struggle.

A New Beginning

It was 1990, less than a month after the reunification of Germany. I was standing in what had been East Berlin, looking westward. The Brandenburg Gate with its heroic figures and massive pillars was being refurbished. The Wall had been demolished. All that remained was a series of light standards that cast a yellowish glow on the dreary area. It was eerie to walk the same section where East German Stassi police had patrolled only months before. Checkpoint Charlie, the East German border guards, the gun towers, the drab, graffiti-scarred Wall, were all gone. Now they existed only in the memories of the people that had experienced them, and in the powerful videos we all saw on television that showed the revolution firsthand. Television had become part of the process. It had documented the seeds of discontent and helped spread them into a full-blown revolution. We were there to show a close-up of the first domino as it fell.

I was with a group of newsmen invited by the German government to observe and report the first effects of reunification. It was the final days of the 1990 election campaign, and Chancellor Helmet Kohl was a heavy favorite to win. The Germans were entering a new life, not knowing where it would take them.

I had a similar feeling that night as I walked the dark, damp streets around my East German hotel. I knew my personal life was on the brink of a change. Beverly had been gone for nearly two years. I relished my forty years with her, but I knew I had to move on. It was one of the most difficult realities I've ever faced. On that chilly, rain-splattered night in East Berlin, I knew I'd made the decision, and Beverly had helped me make it.

More than ten years earlier, Beverly and I had been in Quebec City, Canada. I was doing a series of stories on the growing disputes between the French-speaking Canadians in Quebec and the rest of the English-speaking provinces of Canada. I was filming a report in one of the historic old town squares when Beverly started a conversation with a young couple on their honeymoon. She discovered they were from Los Angeles, and that the bride, Anita, was the daughter of Desmond Hinds, a high school friend of mine. Beverly and I often reminisced about our chance meeting with them and how it was one of the highlights of the Quebec trip.

About a year after Beverly's death, I met Anita and her husband Mark again at a wedding reception. After a few minutes of small talk, Anita became serious and said, "Stan, I want you to meet my aunt. Her husband died a few weeks after Beverly, and I think you two would enjoy knowing each other."

It startled me. I hadn't given much thought to dating again. I tried giving them a vague response, but Anita and Mark wouldn't take no for an answer. Mark gave me a definitive invitation:

"We'll call you after the holidays, and the four of us will have dinner together."

Driving home to Los Angeles that evening, I thought about how strange life can be. Imagine, after forty years, going on a blind date.

Gege Elder and I hit it off right away. We enjoyed talking to each other, being around each other, and it seemed as if we had known each other forever. She was a beautiful, intelligent blonde, slim, vivacious, full of endless energy, a top tennis player, a good golfer, interested in everything.

After being alone without Beverly for almost a year, being with Gege gave me new hope. She helped me put the pieces of my life together. It was on that rainy night in Berlin that I decided that we shouldn't wait any longer. Gege and I should stop looking back to what had been and start moving ahead toward what could be. We needed to get on with our lives and start building a future together.

I arrived back in Los Angeles the night before my daughter Margaret's wedding to Dr. Michael McMonigle at St. Brendan's Church. I was every bit the proud father as I walked down the aisle with my beautiful daughter on my arm. Who would have thought I'd be at my own wedding very soon?

While Gege and I talked about Margaret's wedding the next day, I came out with it. "Now that Margaret's married, what about us? When are you going to marry me?"

She said nothing, but smiled.

"Let's do it right away," I insisted.

"Let me look at my calendar," she said, letting out a delightful laugh.

Like any well-written chapter, it's difficult to find the right ending. But we'd found ours, and, together, we began a new chapter with a fresh page. Our love sustained both of us in our life together.

CHAPTER 21
Rodney King and the Los Angeles Riots

My marriage to Gege brought renewed peace to my life. But that calm didn't extend to the city, which exploded with new rage on the early evening of April 29, 1992. My assignment took me into the skies above Los Angeles to report on the riots that were erupting below. Pilot Mike Tamburro kept our helicopter in a tight circle over Florence and Normandie in South Central Los Angeles. I was sitting next to him, and had a clear view of the rampaging masses on the street below, as cameraman Martin Clancey, strapped into a shoulder harness, hung out of the helicopter with his mini-cam on his shoulder.

We began to get more reports of scattered violence. We watched a barbaric videotape of motorists being ripped out of their cars, hammered, pounded, and chased by rock-throwing men on the ground. My mind still burned with the image of Reginald Denny being pulled from his truck and severely beaten about the head and body with large pieces of cinderblock. Afterward, the attacker danced and flashed a gang sign while, to my utter horror, another person on the street reached into Denny's pocket and stole his wallet.

I peered through my side window as the copter continued to circle in a steep bank. A number of cars moving through the intersection slammed on their brakes and made an abrupt U-turn to avoid the anarchy taking hold of the city. Clusters of people loitered, throwing rocks and bottles at the passing cars. Others on the street were darting in and out of a liquor store at the corner, taking what they wanted. There were no police to protect innocent people who happened to find themselves in the wrong place at the wrong time. The looting, beating, and hysteria continued right below me, and all I could do was watch and report. It was one of the saddest times I've ever witnessed as a journalist.

My mind went back twenty-seven years to 1965, when I covered the Watts riots. Reporting from the helicopter, I couldn't help but draw similarities to those dark days. I remember being grateful for one difference: unlike today's riots, Watts had had fires. Sadly, the past caught up with me when I noticed white smoke in the street. An overturned car had just been torched and was beginning to burn. Within minutes, I saw more smoke pouring out of a liquor store's front windows, where looters were still running wild.

As we circled seven hundred feet above the scene, Martin, who was peering into the viewfinder of his camera, shouted over the radio communications system, "That liquor store is on fire!"

Our pilot nodded and refocused the flight circle so we were right over the smoking corner building below. With the fires came increased bedlam. It wasn't long before large flames were shooting out the doors and windows of other buildings. More cars were overturned and burned.

My thoughts again flashed back to 1965. I remember being in the newsroom and watching pilot-reporter Larry Scheer in the KTLA Telecopter broadcasting the first fire pictures from Watts. My reaction was the same as it had been a quarter of a century ago: *I can't believe this is happening, but I'm afraid it's only going to get worse before we can dream of it getting better.*

By this time, the station had pre-empted all programs and was in full riot coverage. Hal Fishman, Larry McCormick, and Jann Carl manned the anchor desks, Ron Olson was in the middle of the rioting crowd outside police headquarters at Parker Center, and Steve Lentz and Marta Waller were covering other parts of the city.

Fires broke out over a widespread area below our helicopter, and dark plumes of smoke spread quickly in different parts of the city. The streets of Manchester, Vermont, Figueroa, Martin Luther King Jr., Crenshaw, Jefferson, Rodeo, and Century Boulevard exploded with new fires. Our pilot broke off from our tight orbit as we spotted flare-ups in new places and cut a diagonal path across the sky to the next erupting blaze.

Each one was an agonizing sight. The number of fires grew quickly from five or six to a dozen, then two dozen. This was no longer like Watts in 1965, where a few fires erupted in a relatively small area; these conflagrations were burning in all directions, and I wondered where it would end. The targets were much the same now as then: supermarkets, Thrifty Drug Stores, Chief Auto Parts, liquor stores, swap meets, Korean businesses, restaurants, and mini-malls — all miles apart from each other — were ignited under the arsonist's torch.

Many mini-malls were completely wiped out. Firemen couldn't respond to a lot of the early fires because snipers shot at them, so police escorts were forced to accompany the fire fighters for their own safety. Through the hours of horror, KTLA remained on the air. Countless times during the night, I kept repeating to myself: *I can't believe this is happening.* I have lived all my life in Los Angeles and thought I knew it so well.

It was heartbreaking to be above my city, watching it burn down to ash heaps. Many of these buildings had been erected in the last few years, a hopeful sign that, at last, renewal was taking shape: a new shopping center here, a new mini-mall there, an old building rehabilitated across the street with a new business opening up inside. All hope and progress since the Watts fires seemed lost in the chaos of that tragic night.

Each one of these fires not only destroyed the buildings, but the jobs and futures of so many people who lived in the community. Now there would be no work, no places to buy anything, no hope, no future . . . all because of the riots of April 1992.

For years to come, I imagine sociologists will discuss why this happened and how years of barely-suppressed of hate created this ultimate conclusion. There was of course one clear catalyst: in the televised trial of the four officers accused of severely beating Rodney King, the jury announced that they had found the officers not guilty.

Rodney King: How It All Began

It's said that reporters should always expect the unexpected because it happens all too frequently. Because of this, I never take those moments in stride. However when I entered the busy newsroom in March of 1991, I had no idea what I was about to encounter.

I reached into my coat pocket and pulled out my press pass. Our assignment editor, Rosalva Skidmore, looked up from her phone call and waved a greeting. I scanned the newswire copy on her desk while she finished the call.

"Stan, when you get a chance, will you take a look at this freelance video that we got today and see what you think we can do with it? It's an amateur home video, but it is really quite powerful."

It was an unusual request, so I put it in a playback unit right away. I looked at the pictures and felt adrenalin surging through my body. In all my years covering the news, I had never seen anything like this before. Although it had been shot the night before in the San Fernando Valley Foothill Police Division, it looked like something that might have happened in Tiananmen Square in Beijing or in a poor black township in South Africa. I could not believe this was Los Angeles.

The first part of the video was blurred, and it was difficult to tell what was going on. But when the photographer found his focus, I could clearly make out several police officers hitting a man with batons over and over again. The beating continued at a frenetic pace as the man rolled around on the ground. He appeared submissive, but the blows continued. I put the VCR in reverse and watched the blows bounce away from the victim. Then I put it back on play and stared in disbelief and growing horror as they pummeled him again and again.

"How did we get this?" I asked Roslava.

"Some guy shot it from his patio. He wants to sell it to us as a freelance news story," she answered.

I kept running the tape backward and forward. "Are we the only ones who have it?"

"I think so."

"What's the background?" I asked.

"There was a pursuit on the Foothill Freeway, the guy tried to get away. When he finally stopped, he got out of the car and tried to take on the whole force."

Several others in the newsroom had come over and were clustered around the monitor. Everyone wore pained expressions as we watched the videotape playback over and over again.

"Better show this to the police first," I said to Rosalva. "We've got to get their reaction."

The tape had been left off at the main gate by a man named George Holliday. He had heard yelling on the street in front of his apartment, so he got his camera and shot the video. He watched the violent beating unfold through the lens of his camera. Our news director, Warren Cereghino, had watched it many times before I saw it, and he agreed that, as a courtesy, we had to show it to the police department brass before we put it on the air. I called Lieutenant Fred Nixon in the press relations department and told him what we had.

"Bring it down, Stan," he said. "I'll have some of the staff take a look at it with me."

The officers were waiting for me when I arrived at the sixth floor office of Parker Center at about six o'clock that evening. They watched silently as the tape was played and replayed. While their official reaction was calm and noncommittal, they appeared genuinely shocked and angry.

Lieutenant Nixon did an on-camera interview with me and said they were launching an immediate investigation to determine what had happened. He declined to comment on the tape until he had all the details. Theirs was a subdued reaction, but we could use it on the air when we ran the tape that night. Several other high-ranking officers saw the tape before I left that evening, and this gave the department time to prepare for the public outcry that they knew would come after we aired the tape.

"Why don't you suspend everyone involved and then worry about the circumstances later?" I asked. Nixon nodded but didn't answer.

I left a copy of the tape at Parker Center, knowing theirs was going to be a long and embittered night. I caught up with my camera crew so we could drive to George Holliday's condominium in Sylmar. We were anxious to interview the man who had shot the tape. As we entered his condo, I saw his new camera was still in the foam packaging. The camera box was nearby, as well as a scattered pile of videotapes, cables, and connectors. George told me he was just learning how to use his equipment and had shot it only a few times.

"There was an Arnold Schwarzenegger movie filming down the street last week," he said. "I took the video camera and got some shots of Arnold and the other members of the cast. It was good experience and I enjoyed it."

"How did you happen to take this video?" I asked.

His wife answered. "The sirens and copter noise woke me up. I went out on the balcony and saw all the commotion and called George. I said, 'Maybe you should get the new camera. There's a lot going on out there on Foothill.'"

"I found the camera," George said. "It took a little time to get it ready and for me to start shooting. I just followed the action."

George Holliday had no idea of the impact his videotape would have. He hadn't planned to contact a television station because he wasn't sure if anyone would be interested. Then his wife called the Foothill Station the next morning to inquire about the man arrested outside their condo the night before.

"The policeman on the phone gave me the run-around," George's wife said. "He wouldn't give me any information at all. So I asked George if maybe we should give the tape to a news station. I was a little scared about doing it, but we decided to call you because of the way they had acted on the phone."

The Hollidays told us how they watched KTLA and knew we did these late-breaking action stories, so they thought we might be interested. After talking to our assignment desk, they dropped the tape off with the security officers at the KTLA main gate.

I knew this would be a difficult story, that the brutality and violence would offend a lot of people. My sole intent was to be as objective as possible, and not to sensationalize something as devastating as this. My job, as always, was to get the story to the people, so they could make up their own minds. I did the on-camera portion of my story and then went back to the newsroom to finish up the rest.

As we finished putting the report together, we discussed our concern for George Holliday's safety. Would putting his face on the air make him a marked man? How important was his on-camera appearance to our presentation?

While we were getting the tape ready for our ten o'clock broadcast, assistant police chief Bob Vernon paged me over the newsroom loudspeaker. "Stan, I want you to know that we have already sent investigators out to the site where the videotape was shot. They are working in the rain talking to witnesses right now. All we are interested in is the truth. Let the chips fall where they may."

I thanked the chief. I was glad that we had a strong reaction from the police department because now we could tell the viewers what immediate steps the police were taking before we showed the footage. Holliday's tape was brutally powerful and required no voice over. We let it play until to the end, when the beatings stopped. Then we played Holliday's voice describing what he saw. Of course, we had no video of what had gone on before Holliday started recording. The camera wasn't rolling during the high-speed police pursuit down the San Fernando Freeway. The video didn't capture Rodney King throwing off four officers who tried to subdue him after the chase. It didn't come out until the trial that Sergeant Stacy Koon had to use his Taser gun twice in an effort to control Rodney King. With his seemingly superhuman strength, the officers thought King was on PCP.

Rodney King's beating was seen all over the world, and the repeated viewings incited additional anger, rage, sorrow and pain. Even police chief Daryl Gates called it an aberration. It was almost a year until the trial of the four officers accused of beating Rodney King began. There was wide media coverage of the trial, and many stations did live broadcasts from the courtroom. One station, KTTV in Los Angeles, televised the day-by-day proceedings of the entire trial. All the media in Los Angeles and most of the country followed every development of the trial. Those interested in the minute details of the legal arguments had access to the complete story. And, as we all know, defense attorneys were able to raise doubts in the minds of the jurors about the actions they saw on the tape.

A few of the officers involved testified they had been afraid for their lives due to King's unrelenting aggression, even after being shot twice with the Taser. Although there were a lot of officers at the scene, there was the distinct fear they were dealing with a PCP-addled aggressor.

In response, King's defense attorneys talked about "tunnel vision," where a person is so intent on what is happening directly in front of him that he has no idea of his surroundings. The defense also talked to the jury about the escalation of force.

Experts testified that it was necessary to do everything possible, short of shooting, to subdue the man. Lawyers showed freeze frames of the tape, and experts testified that various blows were according to regulation. The jury found three of the accused officers innocent, and were unable to reach a decision on the only remaining count against the fourth officer. Reporters covering the trial rushed to their live cameras, microphones, and computer terminals to tell the world about the decision.

The backlash nearly destroyed parts of the city.

Response and Consequences

Brian Jenkins, a black reporter for KCOP television, and Michael Ambrosini, an anchorman for KNX news radio, were caught up in the surge of violence, and both found themselves playing the unanticipated role of hero in two unrelated and terrifying occurrences.

Brian Jenkins and his cameraman, Bob Quinlan, parked their KCOP camera car on a street in the riot zone and were stunned to see a white man running frantically from four black men who were closing in on him. They tackled the man right in front of Brian and Bob's car, and began to beat him. Bob got graphic footage of Brian opening the door and racing from the truck to pull the assailants off their victim.

Tempers were hot but Jenkins tried to reason with the men. "Come on guys, leave him alone. He didn't have anything to do with the decision. He hasn't hurt anyone. Don't pick on him just because he's white."

The imposing figure of Brian Jenkins balanced his pleas of mercy, and the aggressors grudgingly stepped aside, allowing Brian to place the victim into their KCOP car and rush from the scene. The victim turned out to be a photographer from France who was shooting film that chaotic day in South Central Los Angeles.

I talked to Brian a few days later. "I tell you, Stan, when I saw the videotape that my cameraman shot of me running into the fight, I couldn't believe I did that. I guess something inside of me snapped. I just ran out there without thinking and tried to stop the guys from beating him."

Michael Ambrosini also found himself thrust into a volatile situation as the riots broke out around him near the corner of Vermont and Martin Luther King Boulevard. A microwave television news crew from KCAL-TV was under attack. Reporter Bill Gephardt and cameraman Chris Torgerson were interviewing looters when several men came rushing out of the crowd and chased after them. Gephardt was hit by a flying bottle. At one point he slipped and fell, and the pursuers were suddenly on top of him. He was hit on the side of the face so hard that some of his teeth were nearly knocked out. Some men kicked him viciously in his side while others tried to steal the television camera.

In the fight over Torgerson's camera, Gephardt was able to get up and run through traffic into the middle of the street. The four assailants grabbed the KCAL-TV camera from Torgerson and began to chase after Gephardt. As the two panic-stricken reporters ran through traffic, they spotted Ambrosini's KNX car. The car hardly stopped when the door swung open and both men jumped inside.

Ambrosini tried to pull away but the car got stuck in the heavy traffic. The attackers pounded on the windows, grabbed the locked doors, and shook the van, trying to get at the fleeing newsmen. The moment Ambrosini found an opening, he cut the car free, and the three of them fled the scene. Injured from flying glass, Bill Gephardt had to be taken to a local hospital. The KCAL-TV microwave truck had to be abandoned on the street.

While this was going on, a KTTV television truck also had to be deserted after mobs running through the Fedco Store parking lot spotted the television crew huddled inside the big white truck. The rioters began banging on the doors and rocking it back and forth. People pelted the truck with anything they could get their hands on. One man dealt vicious blows to the windshield and the side of the truck with a two-by-four while shouting at the engineers hovering inside. The glass shattered but didn't break.

The crew had hoped to ride out the storm, but the situation had become desperate, and their only hope was to get out of the area. They tried to start the truck so they could escape the threatening crowd. What the engineers didn't realize was that one of the heavy blows from the two-by-four had hit the "kill switch" — the safety feature designed to shut off the engine if the driver loses control of the vehicle — making the truck inoperable. The frightened crew was now stranded among the rioters, with no means of escape. Thankfully, though, new targets drew the attention of the mob, who lost interest in the truck and turned their attention back to looting. The engineers took advantage of diversion and fled the scene. Abandoning the truck, they found refuge at the house of one of the engineers' grandmother, who lived half a mile away.

For months after the looting and burning, local newsmen spoke of their close calls in the riots. I happened to see Marco Peterson, a black cameraman from KTTV, who had covered the story. He'd turned out to be a hero in the abandoned microwave truck story when he volunteered to go back to the Fedco parking lot days later to try to salvage the truck.

"Stan, did you know that was my son's truck?" he told me. "He had just started working at the station, and I wanted to go down to the Fedco parking lot to see if the truck was still there. I tried my best to blend in while walking through the crowd of looters. So I wouldn't arouse suspicion, I pretended I was stealing the truck. I tried and tried, but the truck just wouldn't start. The battery had died. Since Robert and I had driven down in a big pick-up truck, we decided to push the KTTV truck out of the parking lot. The whole time this was going on, looters were running in and out of the store, carrying anything they could get their hands on. Many simply drove their cars to the parking lot and filled them up with the stolen merchandise. In the meantime, Robert drove the pick-up behind the disabled KTTV truck and started pushing it. The crowd started cheering. 'Keep going, Brother, it's all yours!' 'That's the way. You're taking the big one.' 'Good going. That's what I like to see!' We waved back, left the parking lot, and headed over to a quiet part of the neighborhood where we called a tow truck." Marco then smiled. "The tow truck cost the station fifty bucks. Pretty good deal, don't you think?"

A few weeks after the riots, I was in Simi Valley. About a hundred people had gathered outside the courthouse to denounce the decisions in the Rodney King case, shouting speeches over a loudspeaker. Many were angry, but the rally was peaceful. Local police in riot gear were inside the building and were ready to move into action in case things got violent.

One of my colleagues also covering the story was James Bartholomew, a freelance journalist who often worked for the *New York Times*. Bart was still sporting a badly bruised jaw, a souvenir from the riots. He'd been taking pictures at Florence and Normandie when he got caught in the flash point of the outbreak and was attacked and beaten by an angry crowd. Someone grabbed a large stick and smashed him in the face. Others took his cameras and trashed his car.

A man watching the attack was able to get to Bartholomew and help him back to his car. When other rioters saw this, they attacked the car, pulling the doors open, rocking it viciously, and jumping on top of it. Not only did they almost total his car, they also stole thousands of dollars of cameras and photographic gear. Despite it all, Bart still had his pictures from the start of the riot, and they were published in the *New York Times*. The photos showed police trying to arrest a man while a large, hostile crowd surged around them. Bart had been out of commission for a few days, but now he was back here in Simi Valley, cameras strapped around his neck, covering the news.

There were many heroes among the cameramen and reporters who covered the riots. Many were beaten or had rocks and bottles thrown at them, others had their cameras stolen and their vehicles damaged. At least three of the helicopters that flew over the fires and rioting were hit by gunfire. The KCOP and KNBC copters had bullet holes in their fuselage, and my copter was nicked in the rotor blades by a bullet. But there were no fatalities in the media. The Greater Los Angeles Press Club saluted all of the journalists who covered the riots during the burning, looting and vandalizing. At its 1992 Headliners dinner, it honored "The Media 500," those members of the news media who survived the Los Angeles riots.

The Aftermath

Los Angeles still lives with the scars of those riots, the worst uprising in this country since the Civil War. The charred debris from the fires have been cleared, but to this day, many empty lots remain. Bare, upright, exterior walls still stand, constant reminders of the days of fury. Fifty-three people died in the violence, more than six hundred buildings burned, and damage to the city totaled over $1 billion. It has taken a long time for the heart and spirit of Los Angeles to recover.

CHAPTER 22

6.8 on the Richter Scale: The Northridge Earthquake

On January 17, 1994, a terrifying rumble sent demonic hands bursting up from the ground, grabbing the eaves of my house and trying to rip it apart from its concrete foundation. I knew it would be only a moment before the shuddering walls, shattering glass, and the creaking, moaning roof would come crashing down on us. My wife Gege did the only sensible thing: she pulled the covers up over her head. We were in good company, as millions of terrified Californians were jarred from their sleep to face the real-life nightmare that was erupting from ten miles below the earth.

Gege and I groped for our slippers as we stumbled through the ruin of our home, using nothing but the tiny green light from the base of our telephone as a flashlight. Even in the frenzied moments after the quake, I knew I had to leave immediately for the station. If it was this bad here, it was surely worse elsewhere in the city. The combination of aftershocks and damage could be devastating if Gege were alone, so I persuaded her to spend the day with me. Wearing sweats, one tennis shoe, and one slipper, Gege took my hand and followed me as we felt our way through the darkness downstairs to my car in the driveway.

Los Angeles was completely without power, and darkness enveloped everything as we drove down Sunset Boulevard. I felt reassured seeing the high-rise buildings in Century City still standing. Maybe the damage hadn't been so severe after all.

The station was already on the air with earthquake coverage when we arrived. Hans Laetz, the assignment editor, looked up from his phone call and saw me rush into the assignment room. "Stan, Greg Hunter should be here any minute. Both of you take Unit Ten. Head out to the valley and look for damage. I think we've got freeway problems." He put the phone down and turned to the radio in front of him. "Sky Cam Five, I know it's pitch black out there, but do you see any damage?"

I picked up my reporter's notebook, and Gege and I bolted toward the parking lot just as Greg Hunter pulled into a space. I could feel the electricity in the air as others arrived and ran into the newsroom. It was going to be a long day.

Gege, now sporting a pair of tennis shoes loaned to her by weekend anchor Marta Waller, got into the back seat and sat next to the third member of our crew, Carlos Quintero, who was checking the camera gear. Since everything had only just happened, it was difficult to know where to go. I knew there had to be major damage, but didn't know where. We took the Ventura Freeway through the Cahuenga Pass, past Universal City, and headed towards Reseda.

"Unit Ten, there are reports of freeway damage on the 5 Freeway. Head out that way," Hans barked over the radio.

Greg picked up speed and we raced toward our target. He pointed out the window and said, "There's a fire in the Hollywood Hills."

I reported the fire to the assignment desk, and we changed course, heading in its direction. There were more fires, growing larger by the minute.

One was burning through the entire top floor of a two-story commercial building in Sherman Oaks, and several fire rigs shot streams of water into the blaze. It was still dark as I got ready for my first live cut-in from the field. All of the windows along this section of Ventura Boulevard were broken, and shards of glass and merchandise were scattered everywhere. As I stood, mike in hand, waiting to go on the air, I watched as two people picked up items from the sidewalk and put them back inside the broken windows of the stores. Amazing, I thought. Here's a case of reverse looting.

As dawn broke, the severity of the quake became apparent. Over one hundred fifty mobile homes had burned in Chatsworth, Sylmar, and Northridge, near the epicenter of the quake. Fifty foot geysers of water erupted from broken fire plugs along Ventura

Boulevard and flowed down the street. At another intersection, water bubbled up through the roadway from broken underground water mains. One part of an apartment complex had been picked up and moved three feet off its foundation, before collapsing on parked cars in an underground garage. Piles of bricks and chunks of mortar were strewn on sidewalks and lawns. Broken walls had fallen everywhere. People stood bewildered in front of their homes, too dazed to start the clean up.

Hans' voice came crackling over the radio. "Unit Ten, head for the Northridge Fashion Mall. There's heavy damage there."

We saw more and more damaged structures as we drove to Northridge. Everywhere we went I saw block walls cracked open and lying on lawns and sidewalks.

My radio was inches from my mouth. "We have an unbelievable picture here, Hans."

The Northridge Mall was an eerie sight. The huge parking lot was empty. Bullock's department store was completely destroyed and sat in the middle of the lot like a beached whale. Its tile facade in the front and back had survived, but the entire roof and sides had collapsed. The third floor was resting on top of the first. A few straggly pillars stood in the rubble, but the structure was gone. To see a modern building ripped apart by the sheer force of nature was a shocking sight, and the question kept going through my mind: What would have happened if the quake hit at 4:30 in the afternoon, instead of the wee hours of the morning? There could have been five hundred people in that building.

We had news teams all over Southern California. Warren Wilson did a report from the Newhall Pass, one of the main freeways running north-to-south across the state. The broken spans and collapsed freeway sections were in the same area as the 1971 quake. Marta Waller and her camera crew were at a Reseda apartment complex whose third floor had fallen and crushed the second floor, causing sixteen deaths and many injuries. Bob Navarro reported live on the damaged buildings he discovered in Hollywood, twenty miles from the epicenter of the quake, while Jennifer York's helicopter flew over the devastation.

I was on the air at the climactic moment when firemen freed a mall maintenance worker, who had been trapped for many hours, from the collapsed parking structure of the Northridge Mall. Greg Hunter grabbed his camera and climbed on the roof our truck to show viewers close-up pictures of what was happening.

My next report was from a derailed freight train. It was a jumble of tank cars and boxcars thrown about by the force of the earthquake, some tilting precariously, others completely on their sides. Railroad repair crews worked to remove the wreckage and put as many of the cars back on the tracks as possible. We drove down along the tracks to do our report, but the Southern Pacific police turned us away.

"This is railroad property," they shouted. "You have to get out of here!"

They made it clear there would be no negotiating. Los Angeles police had been helpful all day long while we made our reports and took our pictures, but the railroad workers weren't prepared to have twisted tracks and derailed tank cars filled with hazardous materials splashed across the evening news.

The train had been uprooted under the Nordhoff overpass, which had been closed to traffic after the quake dropped it about a foot at the point where it connected to the bridge. We stopped our camera truck just short of the span. Greg opened the back door and reeled out about two hundred feet of camera cable so we could walk onto the bridge and show pictures of the damaged railroad cars below. Some fifty people were staring at the twisted wreckage as we got ready to go on the air. As is common out in the field, we invariably have to wait our turn before going live to the studio. I was holding my microphone and Greg was standing next to me, lining up his camera, when the damaged bridge started to dance. It was a gentle bounce, but the 5.3 aftershock scattered everyone still standing on the bridge. Except us.

I looked at Greg with his camera. He looked at me with my mike. We agreed to stay without any words passing between us. The span rocked and swayed for only a few seconds, then settled down. Other places weren't as fortunate, and I could see puffs of dust on the distant hills where the aftershock had stirred the ground. Our live report caught great footage of emergency crews in protective gear draining the toxic substances from the overturned tank cars.

We spent the entire day driving around Northridge and its neighboring communities. Everywhere we went, strings of yellow tape circled damaged businesses. Empty parking lots were everywhere, and for the first time in history, the entire city of Los Angeles lost its power supply. There was no water and no place to buy food or supplies. Supermarkets were shut down while employees cleaned up scattered merchandise. Restaurants were closed and gas stations couldn't sell gas because there was no electricity to pump it from their tanks. It was eerie to see the city stagger under the blow, unable to bounce back quickly. Emergency efforts were in full swing, but the day-to-day necessities we take for granted had vanished.

We reported from parks where hundreds of people had congregated, fearful of sleeping indoors. Our cameras and interviews captured buildings that were still intact but had been thrown off their foundations, as well as other buildings that had been consumed by fire. I interviewed many people whose faces wore expressions of severe shock as they recounted their narrow escapes from death.

It was close to midnight. We had been going strong since four in the morning. Gege's hand held mine as she slept in the front seat with her head on my shoulder. Greg napped in the driver's seat, and Carlos sat silently in the back. Dim lights outlined the tilting and burning buildings. Reduced to rubble, they seemed to symbolize the heartbreaking scenes I had encountered throughout that long day.

While we'd spent long hours covering the lives of others, we personally hadn't been impervious to the destruction, and it was now time to take stock of how our KTLA family had fared. Knowing that we have to forgo our own problems in order to do our job is one of the hardest aspects of broadcast journalism. We rush to a scene of tragedy, and somewhere in the back of our minds, we can't help but wonder if our own home survived or if our family members are okay.

My cameraman, Rod Gilmore, who had just bought a home in Sylmar, lost it in a matter of a few seconds. He had saved up for years to make the down payment and had spent all of his spare time fixing it up.

News Producer Ryan Cowen and his wife Nancy watched green, red, and blue explosions fill the sky from the nearby power plant that made daylight out of darkness. It faded and everything went black with the loss of power.

As I did my quake follow-up assignments and read reports of the television coverage of the earthquake, I understood the major role KTLA had played in keeping the entire nation informed. While many of the stations had trouble getting on the air because of the major power failure in Los Angeles, KTLA went to emergency power and continued to broadcast via satellite up-link.

When the networks saw our coverage and weren't able to get pictures from their local affiliates, they asked KTLA for permission to pick up its signal. All three networks, ABC, CBS, and NBC, as well as CNN, broadcast our coverage that day.

For many hours, KTLA's telecast of the devastated areas was one of the primary national sources of news. The public's need to know was the important factor, and it overrode the old constraints of competition and turf protection. The rest of the nation wanted to see what was going on in Los Angeles.

Columnist Marvin Kitman of the New York paper *Newsday* wrote that he was most impressed by the coverage by the local stations in Los Angeles, saying that because of our reporting, New Yorkers got to watch the coverage all day long and become involved in the story.

"You are there, in the tradition of Edward R. Murrow's radio reports from the rooftops during the London blitz. Except this is live and instant," he wrote. "The news today invites you into the stories. More and more we are participants. We are in all the stories as reporters, fire fighters, rescue workers and victims. We are all of them."

Flowers, baskets of cookies, and letters of thanks poured into KTLA from other stations that had used our coverage.

In any emergency operation, response time is one of the most important elements. In television, response time is fastest when you're ready. KTLA always made sure we were ready and, once again, could meet the crisis.

Scientists have told us that, although the 1994 earthquake measured 6.8 on the Richter Scale, the actual vertical ground movement was among the most powerful ever recorded in the history of California.

The damage was, of course, widespread. More than sixty people were killed and 9,000 were injured. The damage estimates went as high as $46 billion. There were 300,000 applications for government assistance following the earthquake, the largest number ever to seek help after a disaster.

Over 55,000 buildings were damaged, 10,000 of them left unfit for habitation. But the city survived.

Soon after the quake, I had a conversation with an architect in an elevator. "I wish you could tell the quake story from our point of view," he said. "It all sounds so doom and gloom. But think of it this way: a 6.8 earthquake hit Southern California, and 99% of the buildings survived."

Los Angeles is disaster prone; it will be ever so. The natural cycle of brush fires, mudslides and floods, high tides and snowstorms, drought, and earthquakes run through our history. Some say it's the price we pay to live here. When you add recession, unemployment, and an unfriendly business atmosphere, you would think the city is coming apart at the seams.

However, it is important to remember that Southern California is the eleventh-largest economic unit in the world. If it were its own nation, it would be ranked just behind the United

Kingdom, Canada, Spain, and South Korea. Almost fifteen million people live in the five-county area, which is greater than the populations of all the other states, except California, New York, and Texas.

It's one of the largest port cities in the country. Some sixty million passengers fly into our airports yearly. Over twenty-five million tourists visit each year. And though some companies are leaving the area, others are coming in. The defense industries are cutting back and restructuring, but we still have more manufacturing jobs than any city in the nation, more than Chicago and Dallas combined.

If you drive the freeways at rush hour, you'll experience traffic jams along with thousands of Californians on their way home from work. They have jobs, homes, families, and opportunities, and they share in the great promise of the city. The vast majority of them are here to stay.

Don't sell Los Angeles short just because so many things have happened to tarnish its image. It has taken its hits, but the damage is far from fatal. This area is a dynamic economic machine that rolls on and on. And if you ask me, it still has more to offer than any other place in the country.

CHAPTER 23

The Nineties and Beyond: Still Chasing Sirens, Stars, and Dreams

As a reporter, I am mostly an observer of scenes, and it's a serious business. But there are times when there's nothing to do but laugh.

Once, I was kneeling behind an old abandoned car in a cluttered vacant lot with a photographer from the *Los Angeles Times*, covering a gunman who had holed up inside a small mom-and-pop grocery store directly across the street from us. Although we were well hidden, our ringside seats allowed us a perfect view into the doorway of the tiny market. For a journalist, it just doesn't get better than that.

As we waited, I looked at the quick notes I'd made: a robbery attempt by a gunman who fired two shots into the ceiling before running into the back of the store. The employees and customers were all able to get out, but everyone was sure the robber was still inside. The police surrounded the store in hopes of preventing his escape.

I looked up from my notes to watch a police sergeant pick up a bullhorn and order the gunman to come out. The only answer was silence. After a long wait, the officers decided to go in and get him.

The photographer and I had been kneeling silently for a long time, hardly moving. As the tension built up around the front door, there was an explosion that sounded like a gunshot. Instinctively, I stood up to run, but as I did, my left leg completely collapsed, and I fell into the dirt behind the car. The photographer whipped around, fear in his eyes, thinking I'd been shot. He reached over to help me get up, and kept asking if I was okay. I was too embarrassed to answer. I used the bumper of the car and to pull myself up. The photographer still didn't know if I'd been shot, and I finally mustered the courage to assure him that I was fine. We'd been kneeling behind that car for so long that my leg had fallen asleep. It gave way when I got up, which was why I fell into the dirt. While my limping around got the circulation back in my leg fairly quickly, the burning in my cheeks took a good deal longer to subside.

We figured out later that the "gunshot" was a backfire from a passing car down the block. At least we were able to laugh about it as we resumed our semi-hidden position. In the end, nothing happened. The officers searched the market only to find that the gunman had already escaped. Nothing to show for the story other than a healthy dose of humiliation. Like I said, sometimes all we can do is laugh. Other times, all you can do is thank your lucky stars.

A High Speed Freeway Pursuit

We reporters are often so involved in the coverage of a story that we lose perspective on what is and what should be. We want the details and often miss the significance. In an instant, in a single flash of time, in a microsecond, the story you are covering can change and you can become the story.

In the summer of 1999, my cameraman Carlos Quintera and I were following several miles behind a high-speed pursuit on a Riverside County freeway. The driver was doing everything he could to out-distance several helicopters and the army of officers who were in pursuit. The freeway chase, which was, mercifully, far from the busy freeways of central Los Angeles, had been going for about a half hour.

Our Ford Explorer was so far behind the driver and the pursuing police that our main job was to monitor the highway patrol radio frequency and listen to the officers as they pinpointed where the chase car was at the moment. I relayed the details back to Sharon Tay, who was reporting the entire event live on the air. I had my freeway map book on my lap while Carlos drove.

We'd been on the air for about a half hour when I heard a loud pop in the rear of our car and instantly knew we'd blown a tire. I looked up from my map as we began to bounce and sway. Carlos wrestled with the steering wheel, trying to regain control. But as often happens, in this case man was no match against machine. Like a wild mustang breaking from its corral, the car tore across the fast lane of the Riverside Freeway.

Carlos gripped the wheel and yelled over the noise, "I'm so sorry, Stan!"

While my brain raced in high gear, the scene unfolded in slow motion. We made a relatively smooth arc across the lanes of the freeway. I didn't see any cars. So far, so good. The only thing I saw was the dirt shoulder of the freeway coming at us, and I hoped we'd be able to stop or regain control before we reached it. No such luck.

The car bounced from the roadway and launched into the air in a cloud of billowing dust and the jarring thunder of breaking glass. Our three-thousand-pound Ford Explorer rocketed into space while all my emotions pleaded, "Abort, abort . . ."

My memories of those terrifying moments are like patchy snapshots. It must be nature's way of sanitizing of pure fear. I remember seeing the windshield break apart and thinking how great it was that it hadn't shattered and cut us to pieces.

The car rolled over three times, cart-wheeling over the barren terrain, and, unbelievably, we somehow ended up in an upright position. Dazed, I looked around our destroyed car as reality gradually rushed in around me. Carlos had nearly been thrown out of the car. All I saw of him were his legs from the knees down, caught in the driver's side window. The rest of his body had fallen outside of the vehicle, and he was hanging by his legs. Had the car flipped over, it would have landed on top of him.

The next thing I recall was strangers running toward us. Even though the car was badly damaged, the passenger cabin was untouched. A fireman who'd witnessed the accident examined me and asked a lot of questions, while two women wrapped a sweater around the bleeding cuts on my head.

The paramedics arrived and kept me calm while the firemen pulled out their power tools to cut the door off. The EMTs gently pulled me out of the wreckage and carried me to the back of the ambulance for a siren-blaring ride to the emergency room.

The staff at Riverside Community Hospital bandaged the back of my head and checked for other injuries, reassuring me every step of the way. Afterward, they gave me a phone to call home and some time to rest.

Later that afternoon I heard the staff talking about the news media gathering in front of the hospital, and I had to laugh. How many times I've stood outside hospitals on stories and, in most cases, I was never allowed to talk to the injured person. But this case was different, and I realized I'd now become the story rather than the one chasing it. I told the emergency room doctor that this patient would be more than pleased to talk to the press and have cameras at my bedside—after all, I was one of them. The doctor was a little surprised but had no objections. In a few minutes I had a room full of cameras and reporters who were all asking me questions about the accident. It was an odd feeling. I'm always on the outside of a story looking in, and to be on the other side of the camera lenses as the center of a news story was unfamiliar territory.

And as for the high-speed pursuit? It turned out to be fairly dull, so the newsmen focused on my accident for their television newscasts rather than going back to their stations empty handed. LOCAL REPORTER INJURED IN HIGH SPEED POLICE CHASE became the headline of the day, and my interview was on most of the stations for their evening newscast.

Carlos and I were extremely lucky. He broke a rib and had to be briefly hospitalized, taking several weeks off work to recuperate. I was back at work the following week.

Strength at the Helm

News is about what's happening today, and it takes the strongest talent to do it right. I have the utmost respect for my former executive producer, Gerry Ruben. Gerry produced his nightly newscasts like a musical conductor, directing each with flair and enthusiasm. He was known for getting involved and demanding the best from everyone.

Gerry constantly told us, "Keep it simple, be basic, and key your copy to the pictures on the screen. Unlike newspapers where readers can stop and look back to check something, viewers have only one chance to get what you want to tell them or they're lost. Your copy should help viewers understand the pictures they are watching. Your writing must help the anchorman be natural. Write for the ear, not the eyes. Read your script aloud, and make sure it sounds conversational. Leave the fancy words for the novelists.

"News is perishable. It becomes less important as hours go by. If it is yesterday's news, it doesn't belong in today's broadcast. You only use a story again if it has moved forward and has a 'today' news peg."

Gerry sat next to the director during the entire broadcast, and paid close attention to detail. It was the difference between a sloppy newscast and one that was smooth, authoritative, and accurate. He directed the presentation from the trenches and responded to the unexpected quickly. His sound news judgment has always been key to the broadcast.

"Be careful about details," Gerry reminds us: "Are the names right? Is the location correct? Are they spelled right? Don't get so busy that you make mistakes. Be fast but be accurate."

A news operation is more than just its evening newscast. It is essential to keep abreast of the technical advancements that have inundated the news business in recent years. Newness has almost become a plague because it often traps you into buying a system or a piece of equipment that will soon be outdated.

Management is still the key for a successful news department. Our station managers through the years—Greg Nathanson, John Reardon, Steve Bell, Mike Eigner, Peter Walker, Tony Cassara, and John Reynolds—have given the news operation the support it needs to succeed. They make the entire operation work, and have kept KTLA remain one of the leading independent television stations in the nation.

The chairman of the board of Golden West Broadcasting, Gene Autry, was the heart and soul of KTLA for twenty-five years. The legendary cowboy was the kind, considerate owner everyone loved. He was a good businessman, but most of all, he was an outstanding human being. When there were problems, he had good people to handle them, but if they couldn't, he was ready to step in with the right decision. Gene Autry helped the news department soar, and later the new owners, Tribune Broadcasting, kept it flying high.

Touching the Stars: John Glenn, 1998

It was still pitch black outside—predawn. I was one of the first newsmen to arrive at Cape Canaveral. Before too long, hundreds of journalists from around the world would be waiting in line to gain entry. I'd arrived early, but got held up because of my trunk; I'd rented the car mere hours ago and had no idea where the latch was. I couldn't get it open, and none of the security guards who clustered around my rental car seemed to be able to, either. As several guards bent over the open doors scratching their heads, a senior guard left his control shack and saved the day by flicking a lever hidden under the dashboard. The trunk popped open, and we cheered our minor victory.

The security men waved me through with a grin, and I drove to the press parking lot about a quarter mile from our television news trailer. Feeling like an unleashed tourist, I gawked at the same big space building that I'd seen in videotapes dozens of times. KTLA had sent me to Cape Canaveral to report on John Glenn's historic second space flight at the age of seventy-seven, and I felt fortunate to be granted yet another brush with history. Sitting behind the wheel and staring at the giant building bathed in floodlights, my mind filled with memories of John Glenn's first space flight.

The lone man in the capsule. The first American to orbit the earth, in 1962. John Glenn's epic flight brought us into a tie with the Soviet Union in our race to space. Now, thirty-six years later, the hero of yesteryear would blast off as a member of the *Discovery* shuttle's crew. The reality of the seventy-seven-year-old senator returning to space electrified the nation. John Glenn, the last of the great American heroes, had bridged the ages.

The pioneer astronaut had previously made only one space flight. It's been said that President Kennedy never permitted him to return to space because if something had happened to him, it would have been a devastating blow to the American space program. Nonetheless, his career spanned the entire development of America's exploration of space, and Glenn followed his military career with a lifetime of public service in the US Senate. The liftoff of *Discovery* would be his triumphant finale.

Although I had been a television reporter for more than fifty years, this was my first live space shot. I watched all the televised images of space flights from the dozens of videotape stories that I'd reported on over the years. I made regular trips to the Jet Propulsion Lab in Pasadena as the Space Age developed and scientists shared their latest accomplishments with reporters. I had experienced televised launches on videotape over and over again as the slim, roaring rockets blasted off on their long voyages into space. This time I would experience everything firsthand, and I felt this was going to be one of the most powerful experiences I could possibly imagine.

However, it wasn't until I stood there on the damp grass of the Kennedy Space Center listening to the voice of Mission Control tolling the final seconds of the countdown that this impact really hit me. As the rockets ignited, white clouds boiled and churned at the base of the rocket. There was an eerie silence during the few seconds it took for the sound to reach me, three miles away.

The blast was enormous. The sound waves generated by the millions of pounds of thrust pounded at my chest and crackled like machine gun fire. In awe, I watched the fiery golden glow of the *Discovery* ride a billowing, white, foaming contrail into the sky. Its ascent was much faster than I'd expected.

Television pictures are vivid and real, certainly, but they can never recreate many experiences. Being there at Cape Canaveral, watching the *Discovery* blast off, was one of those experiences. On television, you hear the deafening roar and see the rockets streak towards the sky. But once the rocket has launched, there's no reference point to gauge how fast, how high, and how true its course is.

As the *Discovery* clawed its way upward, I found myself repeating a small prayer over and over again. "Please Lord, don't let anything happen, keep it going, keep it going, keep it going."

I watched the shuttle's thin streak disappear into the blue void. After a thirty-six year absence, John Glenn was in space once again. The first time he was alone when his small capsule, *Friendship 7*, sat on top of the Atlas Rocket 109-D. That had been before computers could guide him or modern satellites could track him. There were no live television cameras to record him or sophisticated equipment to back him up as he circled the earth. He was a man of the future back in 1962, and he remains a living monument of where we've been and where we are going.

Though I've made my living through sending the real world into living rooms all over the country, sometimes there's nothing quite like being there and watching. Seeing John Glenn touch the stars once more was an experience I will always cherish.

CHAPTER 24
Some of My Most Satisfying Moments

Sigma Delta Chi Broadcaster of the Year Award

Many of the stories I've done over the years I have completely forgotten. Others I'll always remember. Back in 1993, Steve Weinstein wrote an article about me in the *Los Angeles Times*. His headline was 20,000 STORIES . . . AND COUNTING. AT SEVENTY, STAN CHAMBERS SHOWS NO SIGN OF SLOWING DOWN ON HIS NIGHT-BEAT REPORTING FOR KTLA.

The actual number has risen to over 22,000 stories, but who's counting? I've enjoyed many wonderful accolades and honors, and the first of those that stands out in my mind, and meant the most to me professionally, came one night in 1979, when the Los Angeles chapter of the Sigma Delta Chi journalism fraternity presented me with one of its awards.

Now called the Society of Professional Journalists, it presents the Broadcaster of the Year award to working members of the news media. This award doesn't traditionally go to the national anchors or the high-flying network correspondents covering international hot spots, but rather it recognizes and honors the journeyman reporter. Selections are based on those the committee considers the best, and not necessarily the best-known.

Unbeknownst to me, my news director, Lew Rothbart, nominated me. The phone call telling me that I'd won came out of the blue and delighted me to no end. How wonderful to win without even knowing I was in the running!

The awards ceremony was a black-tie dinner held in the Embassy Ballroom of the Ambassador Hotel, sadly the same room where Senator Robert Kennedy was assassinated in 1968. CBS Anchorman Walter Cronkite was the main speaker, Bill Stout of

CBS was the emcee, and NBC's Jesse Marlow presented the award.

KTLA bought tables for members of our news department. My boss, Gene Autry, invited all eleven of my children to the dinner, and, as far as I can recollect, it was the first time all of us had ever been out to dinner together. Someone was always away at school, working, or sick whenever we tried to have a family get-together. At last all my children were finally going to see what their father had been doing all those years instead of coming home for dinner.

Being only one of the many working journalists in Los Angeles, the Sigma Delta Chi award was a huge milestone. For me, the award gave direction and recognition to a long, sometimes tiring career. Many in the business had been perplexed by me. They saw me on the broadcasts each night and believed I did a good job, but they wondered why I'd remained a local newsman for so long. The conventional wisdom is that if I were any good, I would have gone to a network long ago instead of remaining a local reporter. The Sigma Delta Chi award said, in effect, "It's all right to be a local reporter. It doesn't have to be a mere stepping-stone to the networks."

Practical Wisdom

We never know where the tides will carry us in the news business, so it is best to be prepared to handle whatever comes up. If we develop our talents as a general assignment reporter, we'll be ready to handle many of the specialties that could be assigned.

One of the most important things I've always remembered is not to let the story overwhelm me. Even though I'm in the middle of riots, brush fires, earthquakes, or political conventions, the simple questions of who, what, where, when, and why still apply. Answer them, and I have my story. Of course, a reporter also needs the best pictures possible to make it a good report.

I always know that as a local reporter, I'll be covering the smaller news stories of the day. I'll rarely be called upon to get the goods on a local politician who someone has said is on the take, and

I never go into interviews with the attitude that my subject has something to hide.

The reporter must remember he will be meeting his hometown news sources often, so it is important to be fair and considerate. The contacts and relationships I've made throughout the city have helped me become an effective and accepted part of my community scene. The reporter should do what has to be done, but must avoid being arrogant, overbearing, or a bore. A reporter's reputation is established after just a few encounters and, good or bad, it precedes him wherever he goes. If the reputation is bad, it will always catch up to him at the most inopportune time.

That doesn't mean a good reporter can't ask tough questions. I've asked plenty of probing and embarrassing questions, but since I asked them in a direct and gentlemanly manner, I was always welcomed back to do it again the next time. News sources know we have a job to do, and they respect a professional manner. There's no room for temper tantrums, bullying, or badgering.

Looking back over the years, there are few things I would have done differently, but I'm especially pleased and proud that I was able to stay at one station for my entire career. I never considered leaving KTLA because I was so involved in doing my job. Unlike most, I never took the time to ask myself where I wanted to be fifteen years down the line. With eleven growing children, I had no desire to move to another city and, anyway, I always felt a great loyalty to KTLA.

Also, there's always competition between stations. I was on KTLA's team. It was like playing football for Loyola High School or rooting for USC. It was loyalty to a place, a cause, or a dream. That spirit carried over into television for me, and it made my days at KTLA much more than a job.

I remember in the early years, Klaus Landsberg didn't want us to associate with our competition. We were KTLA and they were the "other guys." My station was something special. My job was to do my best to make it even more special, and through good and bad times I have always felt that way.

There is much to be said for loyalty. The spirit makes you an integral part of what you are doing, and adds extra satisfaction when you do something right. I've always felt there was a big "Channel 5" stamped on my forehead that people could see wherever I went. I think the people at Sigma Delta Chi recognized those elements within me and felt I deserved their award.

Hollywood Star

Over the years, I have covered dozens of "Hollywood Walk of Fame" stories. I've elbowed my way through countless clusters of focused cameramen trying to photograph the new honoree, who is more often than not a big star in Hollywood. For some reason, we get our pictures of the celebrity being honored in the courtyard of the Mann's Chinese Theater, formerly known as Grauman's Chinese Theater.

There are always big crowds of people on hand to watch the recipient uncover their star, which has just been permanently inserted into the sidewalks of Hollywood Boulevard. The Hollywood Walk of Fame is a must-see for tourists, a visual history of the motion picture stars who captured the hearts of their audiences. These are the superstars who are famous, loved, rich, and real.

So it came as a huge shock when, in 1982, my news director told me that I was getting a star on Hollywood Boulevard. I was stunned, elated, embarrassed, and confused. How could I, a television news reporter, be honored with a star on Hollywood Boulevard? Does that happen? I'm far from glamorous, so how is this possible? I never found out.

However, on December 1, 1982, almost thirty-five years to the date of my arrival at KTLA, my movie-going children were delighted to see their dad unveil a shiny new Hollywood Walk of Fame star bearing my name. My colleagues at KTLA were supportive and not at all above gigging at my newfound "importance." All told, I have to admit that I really enjoyed the moment.

So if you ever go to Hollywood, be sure to visit the courtyard of the Mann's Chinese Theater. And be sure to go right across Hollywood Boulevard, to the corner on the other side of the street, where you will see my star. To this day, I have a sneaking suspicion that my good friend, legendary Johnny Grant, honorary Mayor of Hollywood, had a lot to do with my getting it.

And, while you're touring, make sure to visit our historic KTLA studios at Sunset Boulevard and Van Ness Avenue in Hollywood. Today, the ten-acre site is the headquarters for Tribune Broadcasting, and is bordered by an elegant colonial building on Sunset Boulevard that symbolizes the legendary era of motion pictures in Hollywood. It is a direct link from the historic silent picture era of the past to the vibrant television world of today.

In 1997, during a magnificent party celebrating my fifty years in broadcasting, KTLA's General Manager, Vinnie Malcom, and another great friend, John Reynolds, named the main office building on the KTLA lot the Stan Chambers Building. The gathering was made up of television industry leaders and personal friends of mine. I even ranked high enough to have the USC marching band in attendance, and they saw fit to serenade us with the USC "Fight On" song.

On top of this, Vinnie Malcom created the Stan Chambers Journalism Awards, which is an annual essay competition that awards cash prizes to senior high school students interested in journalism careers.

Another of my proudest moments was the sign presented to me from Los Angeles Mayor Richard Reardon and KTLA station manager Vinnie Malcom. It came out of the blue, and I was wholly unprepared for the honor. If you look at the corner of Sunset Blvd. and Van Ness, in front of the KTLA Studio, there is a single light pole. It has the seal of the city of Los Angeles on it, and it's a salute to me.

It reads:

"Stan Chambers, Monumental News Reporter.

50 years of distinguished service to the City of Los Angeles."

Proclaimed by Mayor Richard J. Riordan

Jaime Chambers – Keeping the News All in the Family

As I look back on my sixty years at KTLA and relive many of those great adventures that kept my life exciting and rewarding, I am very proud that my grandson, Jaime Chambers, is keeping the Chambers tradition going on the air at KTLA.

Jaime has been an outstanding reporter since joining the station in 2001. He has all of those intangible instincts of a great reporter that include insight and creativity. In his short tenure, Jaime has developed that invaluable, intuitive awareness that, somehow always puts a reporter in the right place at the right time.

But Jaime didn't grow up with the intent of following in his granddad's shoes. His first interest was the medical field, and he spent time as a lifeguard and went through paramedic training before returning to college in Santa Barbara.

Jaime loved being a paramedic, and was invited by a team of medical doctors to join a volunteer mission of specialists who were going to care for native patients on Fiji. He was assigned to a medical unit whose doctors removed cataracts from the eyes of blind mothers. Jaime told me how rewarding it was to watch those mothers gaze at their children's faces for the first time. It was a life-altering experience for him, and the doctors all congratulated him on his professional skills.

There were several California lifeguards on Jamie's trip to New Zealand, and the American team enjoyed meeting the local lifeguards and competing against them in several ocean swimming events. The New Zealanders were demonstrating one of their new rescue boats when a series of huge waves nearly capsized it. A lifeguard who was swimming in the rough water was hit in the chest by the boat's bow. Rescue teams raced into the pounding waves and tried to bring the unconscious lifeguard ashore. He had stopped breathing.

None of their lifesaving efforts seemed to work, and they knew they had only a few minutes left to save him. Jamie, as an outsider, stood next to a rescue ambulance at the scene and watched the futile attempts to help the victim. When it appeared that nothing else could be done, Jamie ran into the surf and told everyone he'd recently been trained in a new technique to restart breathing. They stood aside while Jaime pounded on the lifeguard's chest. It worked, and the lifeguard quickly gasped and sputtered his way to recovery. Jamie had mere seconds, but he saved the lifeguard when no one else could. Beyond everything, he was grateful he'd been in the right place at the right time.

Jaime has always had a nose for timing. When Jaime called me one day and asked if he could come by the newsroom to see what happens in the television news business, I was pleased that he had wanted to see the KTLA operation. I showed him around the news room like a proud grandfather, and I could see his eyes light up at the action of the newsroom. One of the staff noticed Jamie's enthusiasm and suggested that he check to see if there were any internships open at KTLA.

He did, and there were.

Jamie started working in the newsroom at the news assignment desk. He hadn't been at KTLA very long before the tragic events of September 11th hit New York City. Like the rest of us, he was caught up in the emotional exhaustion that overwhelmed everyone in the marathon coverage of the terrorist attack. It wasn't long before he proved himself a valuable member of the KTLA news team.

Another time Jaime's quick thinking proved useful was in 2003, when an airplane crashed into an apartment building in the Fairfax area of Los Angeles. He was having lunch several blocks away and raced over to offer his help with the rescue effort. Since he'd arrived before the paramedics, his medical experience came in extremely handy. Unfortunately, the pilot died, and it became a recovery rather than a rescue.

A live KTLA mobile unit arrived on the scene shortly after Jamie. Since reporter Ted Garcia knew Jaime had the facts about the accident, he introduced Jaime to the television audience and had him explain what happened and the role he'd played in the rescue.

"This is my assistant producer, Jamie Chambers, who was here shortly after the crash." He then turned to Jaime. "Jamie, what was the situation when you arrived?" He handed over the microphone and, with that, Jamie became a reporter, live and on the air.

The combination worked well, and Ted and Jaime ended up sharing the on-the-air reporting job for the rest of the hour-long broadcast, passing the microphone back and forth. While one reporter remained in front of the camera telling viewers the story, the other sought out more information and tried to find witnesses who saw the plane crash into the building.

The long afternoon ended, and Jamie had successfully reported his first live television news story. Everyone at the station was impressed at the way he handled the difficult and emotional story, and it launched him on the road to becoming a television news reporter.

To that end, news director Jeff Wald decided to have Jamie go out with me on my news assignments for a six-month period. Of course, I was thrilled with the plan, and I knew his shadowing me would put him in the middle of countless stories, as well as offering firsthand experience in how to prepare those stories for television.

I never doubted that Jaime would make a great start. On one of our first joint stories, we were assigned to cover the funeral for a high school boy who was killed in a shooting. The entire student body attended the service at a local church. It was a heartbreaking assignment, and none of the hundreds of students at the funeral service wanted to talk to us. We split up to increase our efforts. About ten minutes later, Jamie showed up with the basketball coach and three teammates who had all agreed to be interviewed. Theirs was a moving tribute to the boy and, because of Jamie, we were able to get their story on the air.

As Jamie's short tenure went on, he proved himself to be a good field reporter and a determined newsman who could gather all the elements of a breaking news story. And, best of all, he was always ready by airtime.

A perfect example of his skills occurred during Jaime's coverage of a high-speed chase and shooting by a deputy sheriff in San Bernardino County. The investigation was underway when the

KTLA crew arrived at the shooting scene. The cameraman filmed the video while Jamie interviewed police officials and various witnesses who were in the crowd. He discovered that someone had a video camera and had taken footage of the actual shooting. It took Jaime quite a while, but he was able to track down the amateur cameraman a short distance from the shooting scene. The man still had the camera with him, and Jamie asked him to play the tape and let him see what had happened.

The video was graphic and quite damning, and clearly showed the deputy sheriff shooting the victim. Jamie bought the video from the cameraman, and it played on our news broadcasts many times during the carious follow-up stories. Based on the video, Jaime's team was able to put together many of the facts of the story. His good reporting and solid facts created an outstanding series of stories for our news broadcasts. The icing on the cake was when Tribune Broadcasting honored Jamie and his crew with a major national award for their coverage of shooting.

A Special Note from Jaime Chambers

Between my grandfather and me, we have sixty-six years of news experience. I have six, and well, he has the rest. All of our coverage has been for the Tribune West coast flagship station KTLA.

My entrance into reporting was as accidental as everything else in my generally fortuitous life. One day I awoke restless in my Santa Barbara apartment—my girlfriend, Julie, was in class, I was waiting for an acceptance letter from a paramedic school I'd been fighting to get into, and, worst of all, there was no surf. It was one of those listless days where I felt there was great potential out there if I could just get off the couch. The best way to get myself moving was to see my grandfather, Stan Chambers.

Stan is a news icon of the West Coast, but to us, his family, he's Papa. Even though we're family, he's a very busy man, and sometimes the best way to get some quality time with him few hours is to meet him while he's reporting and ride along. Since I had always been intrigued by my grandfather's larger-than-life job, I roused myself and called him to ask if I could pop in for a visit.

As I bounced along the 101 Freeway the next day in my old green Ford Bronco, I felt a determined excitement that I couldn't explain. I'd ridden with Stan before, so what was so different this time? As I thought about the weightier issues of providence biting my backside, my beloved truck started to smoke and spit. I pushed on, hoping it was just a minor problem, but the clouds of exhaust billowing from my tale pipe forced me over to the side of the road. On most days I would have just called a cab and gone home, but something told me to keep pushing on.

After getting a tow, I went to rent my first car. The large, pasty woman behind the counter told me I didn't have any credit history. I was only twenty-one; of course I didn't have any credit history. I had to cajole her with my emergency technician card, my Del Mar life guard badge, and my college ID before she finally relented and agreed to rent me the last lime green Dodge Neon on the lot. I raced to the station in my new set of wheels, but I missed Stan by a few minutes. Damn, this news stuff is hard.

Stan's colleagues gave me the address where the story was taking place, and told me Stan was working on a triple homicide in Simi Valley. When I got to the neighborhood, it looked like a movie set, with satellite trucks, news vans, and cops crowding the small streets. Stan was standing off in a corner, away from the madness, looking peaceful but concerned. When I walked up to him he gave me a sly look and said, "You've done half the job; you found us." Then he walked away.

I realized later that he wasn't ditching me, but doing what he does best: waiting to be recognized by a witness and letting them come to him without the fear of hundreds of cameras bearing down on them.

Stan's reporter lesson #1: Don't scare off the witnesses; most of the time they've already been through a lot.

It was great to see this lesson in action as a man from the neighborhood quietly edged up to Stan and chatted with him for a while before agreeing to an interview. When the crowd of reporters saw the man talking with Stan, they rushed over with their cameras blazing. Frightened, the witness fled back to his house and refused to speak to anyone else. Luckily, Stan had gotten what he needed, and he was the only one who had an eyewitness statement for the news that night.

The rest of the day I tagged along while Stan and his cameraman, Carlos Quintero, chased heavily-armed police officers who were pursuing various leads on the murder suspect. We watched the police tackle a man in a field who turned out to be a gardener holding a rake. At the end of the day I was exhilarated and, on a whim, signed up for an internship at KTLA.

Stan told me I had to wear a suit at all times, adding, and I quote, "The good part is, if it gets really hot you can even take off your jacket." How I'd wished he'd been kidding. Because my duties were restricted to stacking hundreds of tapes on my hands and knees, keeping my jacket on was more than uncomfortable for this sweaty intern. My first official day at the station was Monday, September 10, 2001. Stan marked the special occasion by undergoing hip surgery.

The next day, America woke up to 9/11. The normal rules of the news room went right out the window, so we could keep up with the crisis. News directors were running tapes to editors, news writers were directing the anchors, and interns were producing. I was ordered to edit a montage of video clips showing firefighters pulling people out of the mangled wreckage of the twin towers. It didn't take long before I was completely lost and wondering what to do next. After some questions to the staff, I was on my way. Who knew Stan's grandson could produce?

Between the moments of disbelief caused by the attacks and with the adrenalin of my editing the footage, I spent the day vacillating between panic and clarity. We edited out some of the footage because it was so graphic. Even with my emergency medical background, my stomach turned at all the horror. The montage was set to Whitney Huston's version of "The Star Spangled Banner," and they aired it nearly a dozen times. For America, there were no winners on that tragic day. On a personal level, however, I like to think I did a good job of capturing the faces of the brave first responders fighting to save lives in the most disastrous of conditions. It was then that I knew I'd chosen my profession.

Papa was great at giving advice. I remember he told me one day, "Stand where lightning is most likely to strike." He always seemed to stand in the right places, but could I? Did I have that gift? I got my answer a few months later when an airplane crashed in the Fairfax district. I'd like to say that it was my gifts of insight that put me in the right place at the right time, but in keeping with Stan's reporter lesson #2: Full disclosure, I have to admit that I had just finished a margarita at a Mexican restaurant when the plane struck the apartment complex. My brother Willie and I saw helicopters swarming overhead, and decided to see if we could help.

As we approached, I could see people jumping from the second story windows and victims lying on the ground. Since the emergency crews hadn't arrived yet, I started a medical assessment on a man who appeared to be having a heart attack. Once the medics arrived, Willie and I were relieved of our medical duties.

As we turned to leave, KTLA reporter Ted Garcia, recognized me from the station and pulled me in front of the camera. "This is Jaime, our producer, and he is going to tell us what is happening."

I thought to myself, what the hell am I going to say? So I just pretended to be my grandfather, and in my best 1950s reporter voice, I said, "The plane smashed in to the building and now the apartment complex has been completely gutted. It's a fluid situation . . ."

Because of that story, Ted won an Emmy and I got a job. Later I thanked Ted for the huge on-air promotion from intern to producer. After reporting that day, I went back to the station and the general manager called me into his office. I thought I had done something terrible and was about to be fired. Vinnie Malcolm asked me, in his cool Jamaican accent, where I wanted to go in this business. I replied in a shaky voice, "I want to do exactly what my grandfather does."

He smiled and waved his hand. "Get out of here." As I turned to leave, he said, "Let's make it happen." When I think back to that moment, it still feels like I was watching it on a film.

My biggest advantage in getting into the news business was not my last name, although there's no denying it helped. But my real edge was the advice my grandfather gave me on those hard days when nothing was going right. In general, when there was a crisis involving internal bickering with coworkers, he would tell me to say nothing, continue about my job, and let everything pass. Other times he would tell me to take immediate action to address certain problems. His advice was priceless, and his judgment was perfect — even when he refused to talk to the boss to help me get a remedial job on the assignment desk.

I asked him, "Can't you just help me get that ten dollar an hour job?"

He shook his head. "No. If I get you your first job, you will never be able to work in this business with any credibility."

At first I was hurt, but later I realized he was right again.

Stan Chambers is legend in the reporting world of Los Angeles, but more than that, he is a legend in the way he has lived his life. He's never been petty or angry. His lessons about staying calm when deadlines are looming and turning the other cheek to those who would try to harm your career have been invaluable in my life. But the best part of working with Stan is I get to see Papa every day.

EPILOGUE
Breaking News

Longevity is the ability to adjust to the present and change for the future. It is the ability to hold onto dreams and continue to work in the world of reality. I've lived my dream by spinning in the vortex of the news tornado. There has been little time for my personal observations, and I've spent sixty years trying to be the unbiased reporter, borrowing heavily from Jack Webb's famous admonition on *Dragnet*, "Just the facts, ma'am."

Through the years, I've covered the breaking news stories— from storms, explosions, air crashes, floods, murders, depressions, riots, freeway openings, and high-speed chases, to the occasional high school and college graduation. These events tell their own stories. They are the essence of reality. I have always hesitated to add my editorial observations. The event is there for all viewers to see, and my personal comments often seem extraneous. So over the years I've kept my own opinions mostly to myself. Until now.

Television news reporting is a twenty-four hour a day job, and there is no overtime pay. It starts early in the morning at the assignment desk, where we wrestle with the daily challenge of getting our news crews to the scene of the major local stories, and can last into the wee hours of the next morning. A reporter is on a continuous search for what is happening because news stories are arrogant partners that can deceive us. They can fall apart in the blink of any eye, leaving us with unusable video and no story. Every trip out into the community demands our full attention, and we have to be ready to go at any time.

The news business, for me, is almost an addiction. I begin my day by scanning the morning newspapers and juggling the random flow of evolving stories as I prepare for the newscasts each night. In between, I listen to the emergency radio transmissions that alert me to any breaking news stories.

It's the challenge of getting the story and knowing that most of it hinges on luck, creativity, and determination. And at the end of the day, when the evening broadcast goes well, there is that sweet reward of personal satisfaction, knowing that I helped make it happen, that I'm a small part of a very big whole.

Changing World

For many years, the most exciting sound in our news world was the ringing of five bells on the old UPI teletype printers. In the early days, the teletype machine was the symbol of what news reporting was all about. It was the source, the news alert, the call to action. *Something has just happened! Here is what we know. . . . More news to follow. Reporters, get going!*

Those bells charged the news room atmosphere. They sent dozens of us racing to the scenes of a breaking news story. Those five ringing bells are, in fact, what started my love affair with the news business. It was a call to arms, a dramatic demand to stop everything and get out there.

I miss the clatter of the teletype machines. It signaled the blend of urgent raw information and a demand that you react to it. Now, it's the computer screen that has worldwide contact with news sources. Everyone in the newsroom has immediate access to the world. The boundaries no longer exist, and video sources are available to all.

Today there are a dozen monitoring devices in the news room. Each one of them can alert us to a breaking news story and provide us with a constant check on demanding stories. It's effective and efficient. But I still dream about the old teletype machine, and the exciting moments it created with its bells.

I spent a lot of years in the KTLA news room before I reached my goal of becoming a reporter, and there were a lot of steps to climb before I finally made it. In those early years of television, there was much to be done. I spent time in production, sales, and public affairs, and I even had a cooking show. From there, I did a stint as national sales manager and made sales trips to New York and Chicago before returning to my first love: newscasting. Doing a little bit of this and a little bit of that was great training, and it helped me move up the ladder at the station because I had the reputation of being flexible, cooperative, and creative.

I think my ability to go from one job to another and do whatever my boss needed the most helped enhanced my longevity. Whenever there was a new job to do, the familiar call came out: "Let Stan do it!"

A Special Note from Stan's son, Dave Chambers

When I was a kid, I can recall an air of intense competition and even a spirit of resentment fermenting between KTLA Channel 5 and the competing local station that sat across the street. While visiting my dad at the station one day, the two of us walked across the street to get a snack off the lunch truck that was parked at the other station.

There they were; the enemy! I was ready for anything and stood waiting for the cue to unfurl my best snob-faced scowl.

I looked up at Dad, who was the picture of goodwill. His bright smile accompanied his warm greeting to everyone in the parking lot. I was confused. Had he forgotten this was the enemy?

Of course, he hadn't forgotten. He simply found it easier to stay true to his values. I did a fair amount of slinking around that day, but I never forgot the lesson. Dad taught me that the best way to move through life is with kindness, integrity and honor. It's a lesson that I've tried to remember every day.

As I grew up, I discovered there is a large community of Stan watchers, people of all ages and backgrounds, who continue to embrace the legacy of a man who communicates beyond his words. His knowledge and dedication are the elements that have always provided continuity and solace in a complex world. It's these aspects that have made working on this project such a joy and honor. Dad, my wife Deb, and I poured through countless memories to tell the unique story of how Stan Chambers and KTLA television grew up together. It is our hope that you enjoyed the journey.